SEATS OF SUICIDE

A DAUGHTER'S PERSPECTIVE

J. M. MURRAY

First published by Ultimate World Publishing 2023
Copyright © 2023 Jodi Murray

ISBN

Paperback: 978-1-922982-54-4
Ebook: 978-1-922982-55-1

Jodi Murray has asserted her rights under the Copyright, Designs and Patents Act 1988 to be identified as the author of this work. The information in this book is based on the author's experiences and opinions. The publisher specifically disclaims responsibility for any adverse consequences which may result from use of the information contained herein. Permission to use information has been sought by the author. Any breaches will be rectified in further editions of the book.

All rights reserved. No part of this publication may be reproduced, stored in or introduced into a retrieval system, or transmitted in any form, or by any means (electronic, mechanical, photocopying, recording or otherwise) without the prior written permission of the author. Any person who does any unauthorised act in relation to this publication may be liable to criminal prosecution and civil claims for damages. Enquiries should be made through the publisher.

Cover design: Rocky Scavone - www.bosspp.com.au
Layout and typesetting: Ultimate World Publishing
Editor: James Salmon

Ultimate World Publishing
Diamond Creek,
Victoria Australia 3089
www.writeabook.com.au

In Loving Memory of

Carol

"Your mum is dead."

"She took her own life."

"A farmer found her when he was doing his rounds this morning."

With Gratitude To:

Shelley

A fierce heart of inspiration.

Blessed be the souls that have fallen your way.

Rocky

For your support, understanding and

"Because You're You"

Contents

About the Author   1
From the Author   3

SECTION 1: MY MUM, CAROL 7
The Promise   9
The News   13
The Viewing   17
The Funeral   21

SECTION 2: A LITTLE OF MY EXPERIENCE ... 29
Life With Dad   31
Life With Mum   43
The Sister   51
A Friend & His Sister   57
Breaking the Cycle – My Way   61
The Pact   65
The Weapon   69

SECTION 3: OUR POWER AS HUMANS 73

Common Obstacles	75
The Blame Game	83
Judgement	91
Toxic Relations	97
The Power of Perspective	103
Emotions – Recognise, Respect, Respond, Reflect, Release	111
Communication Needs Comprehension	119
Threats Must Have Consequences	125
Conscious Change	131
Age Appropriate	135

About the Author

Jodi Murray was born in Victoria and now resides on the Gold Coast in Queensland, Australia.

Jodi's mother committed suicide in 1999, leaving her feeling abandoned, isolated and traumatised. After many years of dealing with the consequential effects of this and encountering her own life experiences that resulted in Jodi needing to manage the complexities of CPTSD, she has decided to document the perceptual strategies that she has utilised to improve the relationship with herself and her relations with others.

Jodi does not have formal psychological qualifications, but the strategies that she presents concentrate on human behaviours and perceptions that every individual can adopt to help themselves and others to overcome a multitude of general mental health and relational challenges.

Seats of Suicide

Jodi has created Seats of Suicide with the hope to empower individuals within their own sense of self. To recognise and harness individual powers and abilities that impact personal, familial, societal and generational mental health fitness and resilience.

Seats of Suicide is her SOS to humanity.

www.jmmurray.com.au

From the Author

This book is divided into three sections. The first two parts of this book have been created to give some perspective to the reader that as a human being I am aware of the struggle, weight and complexity of such an existence. I have experienced the weight of human emotions and understand the complexity of navigating this journey of life with little direction or understanding on what it is to be human.

In trying to convey these details and understanding that, for some readers, some information could be deemed as triggering, I have attempted to provide understanding without descriptive detail.

The complexity of navigating relations with myself and others has provided challenges and taken me in unexpected directions. Perceived nightmares have sometimes turned into fortunate opportunities, while conversely, situations initially deemed to be wonderfully elative experiences have turned to nightmares littered with destructive consequences.

Through experience, I understand what it feels like to be useful yet worthless, required without being wanted, accepted for what I can do, whilst being rejected for who I am. To be deemed insignificant whilst providing others with significance.

I have smiled whilst in the grips of depression and shown strength whilst feeling weak. My perceived strengths often became my weaknesses. I know what it is to feel different, whilst knowing I am the same. I have experienced confusion in apparent transparency and found clarity in murky obscurity. I know the desperation of having nothing and the loneliness of having nobody.

Throughout my journey, I have battled with varying degrees of mental health fitness and consequently been an inpatient in psyche wards and treated as an outpatient on numerous occasions. I have utilised numerous therapies, prescription and non-prescription substances, psychiatrists and psychologists. I have attended sessions with a multitude of practitioners of both formal and informal education and qualifications.

Although this book is a culmination of my exposures to a multitude of life experiences, relations and situations, ultimately it is my attempt to express that as humans, our

From the Author

courage is in our ability or willingness to discover, share and express our individual vulnerabilities.

The final part of this book has been created to bring an awareness to the power and abilities we all possess, as individuals, to establish and maintain a greater level of resilience, improve our own mental health fitness, and establish and maintain improved relations with ourselves and others, therefore contributing to the overall resilience and wellness of our species.

SECTION 1

My Mum, Carol

The Promise

The house is quiet when I wake up. As I make my way into the kitchen, I hear the familiar engine hum of the ZH Ford Fairlane. Remembering Mum was going to get material to make her wedding dress, I rush out to catch her before she leaves to say goodbye. I see Mum sitting in the driver's seat. My eyes are drawn to a blue hose wedged into a small gap in the window. My eyes follow the hose and see it connected to the exhaust pipe. I run to the car.

"What are you doing?" I scream, pulling at the locked drivers-side door, bashing on the window.

Her head lifts slightly in my direction as she slips in and out of consciousness. It's the only response she can give.

Pulling on the hose from the window is unsuccessful so I leap to the back of the car to pull the hose off the exhaust pipe.

I scream at her to "open the door" but she is not conscious enough to respond to me or open the door. Managing to break the window, I drag her out of the car.

With the help of a neighbour, we drive her to the hospital. I sit in the back seat with her, trying to keep her conscious by slapping her face every time she seems to drift further into unconsciousness. On arrival at the hospital, I notice how red her face is from where I slapped her as she is placed on a stretcher by staff and wheeled into the hospital. As the adrenaline fades, a numbing shock invades.

Trying to fathom what had unfolded seemed impossible. My mum was planning to marry in a few weeks and had asked that I walk her down the aisle. Life seemed almost blissful for her. I had finished my recovery faster than expected and was moving out just prior to the wedding. Confusion reigned, memories of her adopted daughter returned, and anger began to replace the shock of the morning's events. How *could* you?

A few days later, when I came home from work, I was advised she had been discharged from the hospital and had decided to stay in the caravan at the back of the house. Embarrassed by her actions, it was her way of taking the time and space she felt she needed. I had been unable to see her during the days at the hospital as she had refused all visitors. I made my way out to the caravan intent on receiving an explanation.

The Promise

Making my way into the caravan, I felt a rush of guilt for the bruising I had inflicted on her face. The guilt was quickly swept away by the familiar anger that had increased during her hospital stay. The anger rapidly turned to sadness as I looked into her deep dark brown eyes and felt a depth of sorrow and sadness I had never felt before. My determined, strong mum looked fragile and broken. Her beautiful face, now withdrawn.

"What happened? What went wrong? Why would *you* do *this*? Of all things? You *know* how this shit feels, you *know* this isn't right. Were you really going to leave me? Did you not think how *I* would feel?"

With an explanation that "perhaps she was worried about finally being happy" and "maybe things just got a little too overwhelming" her answers sounded more like rehearsed therapy scripts than genuine reasons for such a decision. Her fragility demanded that I accept her explanation and allow her to concentrate on moving forward instead of satisfying my endless questions. I left her to rest after we agreed we would talk again the following day.

When I made my way into the caravan the following day her eyes were a little brighter above the still noticeable but fading bruised cheeks. I could still feel her embarrassment at the situation, and I had been endlessly trying to figure out the best way to approach her to deal with the subject.

Not wanting to make her feel worse, I also could not ignore the topic altogether. I wanted to provide comfort, but I did not want to condone her behaviour. I wanted to respect her privacy, yet was desperately seeking satisfactory answers to alleviate my own fears.

Her statements of "a weak overwhelming moment", "maybe I'm afraid to be happy" and "I'll be ok, the doctors helped me" were not sufficient for me.

An hour after talking about anything she would allow, making sure she had a full understanding of how I felt and that I could not bear to lose the only person I truly needed in this world, I finally received the only words that could ever provide me with positive assurance. "I am sorry, I promise I won't ever do this again."

That was it! The feeling of relief swept over me. This nightmare could be put to rest.

My mum NEVER broke her promise to me, EVER.

A few weeks later, I walked her down the aisle. The entire situation seemed like a distant memory.

The News

Everyone is busy in the meat department, ready for opening. As usual the barbeque is fired up and ready to cook the meat for the daily department breakfast. It is a welcomed perk of the job that helps to make the early mornings and cold conditions somewhat more worthwhile. The kettle is on, ready for the habitual coffee. I am mindlessly wrapping the last of the trays to be put in the display case when the department head calls my name from the door. I had noticed the blue uniforms just outside the department without much interest. There were often instances where shoplifting needed to be reported and the local police would attend to take statements from the relevant staff members.

"These officers need a word with you." Instead of resuming normal duties, the manager steps to the side.

"Your mum is dead."

Seats of Suicide

Annoyed, I instantly correct the officer. "Uh no, you mean my future mother-in-law, she has been battling cancer."

I had recently celebrated getting engaged. We had been dreading hearing the inevitable news that her fight with cancer had been lost. Most visits consisted of a cup of tea and attempts to provide comfort by gently massaging the protruding bones that constantly ached. The obligatory funeral arrangements had already been discussed, decided and put into place.

"No. Your mother, Carol." The officer is quick to correct me.

"No" I insist. "I spoke to Mum last night."

"I'm sorry, it is your mother, Carol." His words echo.

"But how? When?" I stutter. His words were not making sense.

"Suicide, your mother took her own life. Her body was found a couple of hours ago by a farmer doing his rounds." I feel the manager's hand on my shoulder. The officer continues, "Is there someone we can call?"

"But I spoke to her just last night! She was happy! This cannot be right. Mum said she has confirmed her availability to be on the committee for the Quarter Horse Championships next year."

The News

The two-hour journey to her home was made in stunned silence. It felt more like five hours.

Turning into the driveway I am reminded this home was meant to be her happily ever after place. Finally settled enough to marry "her knight in shining armour" after many years of vowing to never marry again. Only eight months prior, I had walked her down the aisle for her second marriage. We had discussed the turnaround of her views on getting married again and although I knew very little about the man she intended to marry, she was convinced this was right for her.

Walking into the backyard, passing the beautifully tended vegetable garden I am reminded that yet another of her long-term goals is successfully underway. Home grown, fresh produce.

Turning to walk in the back door, the clothes on the line immediately issue a jolting reminder of why I am here. Holding onto the knowledge that Mum never leaves her washing out longer than necessary, I take the washing off the line and go inside to fold and separate the ironing.

Walking down the hallway, turning into the loungeroom, my eyes are immediately drawn to Mum's handbag. The words chokingly escape, "She would never leave her handbag, so she will be back".

Seats of Suicide

I hear an echo in my words and fall into the comfort of her couch. I will wait!

The Viewing

The life I had worked hard for in recent years became irrelevant. Overcoming addiction and violence in my short life so far, now provided little pride or comfort. I had a whole new world to make sense of and was incurring responsibilities I had never imagined.

The beloved and cherished ZH Ford Fairlane had been returned to the property on the back of a tow truck. I was bitterly aware of the lack of damage to the vehicle. At first sight, nothing was amiss.

Sitting in the passenger seat, my mind was flooded with the memories and cherished moments in this very vehicle. Our girl trips to the snow. The many hours spent together going to and from orthodontist appointments. The apt timing of learning to drive and the ensuing emergency of a bee sting in the crown of her head, which meant I needed to drive to get her to the town hospital during the near fatal allergic reaction….

On searching through the car for anything to help this make sense, I found the blue hose was still inside and there were empty scotch and cola cans. I angrily wrapped up the hose and placed it in the shed. I was sure I had previously thrown the same blue hose into the garbage and a feeling of déjà vu washed over me. The faint smell of scotch churned my stomach when discarding the cans.

Interrupting my thoughts, a police vehicle pulled into the driveway. Momentarily, the hope of hearing this was all a case of mistaken identity prevailed. I was rapidly bought back to reality when the officer stated that as a formality, the body needed to be identified at the morgue. At this moment, I was still holding onto the vague possibility that they had the wrong person.

With her widower driving, the journey to the morgue was made in silence. I did not want to leave the farm, still holding hope that Mum would return home. The handbag was still by her chair in the loungeroom.

Entering the carpark of the morgue felt surreal. Walking into the morgue, I was painfully aware that this was the moment when the waiting game would be over. Any sense of hope was rapidly being replaced by dread and panic.

The Viewing

The police officer led the way to the viewing room. In the window, there was a man in a white laboratory coat looking to the officer for the go-ahead. This scenario seemed all too familiar for them. I felt like I was going through the motions in a gruesome horror movie.

"Are you ready?" questioned the officer.

Wanting to scream no, my body was tense and shaking. I nod dutifully to give my permission for the reveal.

Somehow, I pictured this scenario much differently. I had convinced myself that I would be able to identify the body as not being my mum. I had an expectation that I would be able to touch her, cuddle her, talk some sense into her. Instead there she was, in a small white room, laying on a cold, hard steel table. We were separated by a window of glass. A white sheet covered her body to her shoulders. Her once beautiful olive skin, void of make-up, was now a disgusting orange. Her hair, always impeccably styled and curly, was now lifeless and straight. I longed to see her squinting her eyes shut, as a sign of some life. Instead, they were peacefully closed. I wanted to smash through the glass, grab her and shake her, yell at her to wake up. Instead, I mumbled, "It's her". The curtain closed.

My mum's first broken promise, was also her last.

Her widower caught me as I collapsed to the floor.

The Funeral

The ensuing days passed like a slow, miserable, foggy nightmare. I was unprepared for the questions now cast my way all at once. No suicide note had been found. To my knowledge, there was no last will of testament and there were definitely no funeral arrangements in place. Any family relatives that may have been in contact with Mum were in Western Australia. Mum was my only family and support. I did not have a plan nor the leisure of time to make one. At 18 years old, I felt way out of my depth.

Questions such as the type of casket, handles, colours, materials, linings were overwhelming. What is your funeral budget? What sort of funeral service? Music? Open casket? Types of flowers? A final outfit? Speakers at the funeral? A eulogy? I was drowning in the bombardment of so many details that I had no idea about.

Buried or cremated? I was relieved to be able to answer one question with confidence. Cremation. It had been another one of our silly joking conversations we had had on one of our trips to the orthodontist that neither of us wished to be "buried with the worms".

Then there was trying to notify everyone and anyone. Where to start? I only knew of a couple of close friends. The responsibility of ensuring I notified everyone was heavy. I did not know "everyone", so it was a case of starting at the beginning of her address book through to the end. Every single person I called was genuinely shocked. If nothing else, the Carol these people knew was one of the strongest and most determined women they had ever met.

As a teenager being placed in a convent was one of her earlier challenges and with that came the determined resourcefulness that was to become apparent throughout her life. Escaping the convent by tying bed sheets together to scale the building out of the window but failing to grasp the actual height of the building had her questioning her great escape. Falling the last metres to the ground, she was grateful for a discarded bus seat to soften the fall.

Obtaining a pilot's licence through the Victoria Police during the 1970s was one of her proudest moments and not an achievement too many women could boast about at that time. Undertaking training as a stunt woman. Travelling around the USA as a lone female, sleeping in her car when

The Funeral

necessary was met with "you crazy Aussie lady" many a time and earned her a great deal of respect. Focussing on dreams and achieving was her way of dealing with a messy divorce and custody battle that she never really had any hope in "winning". Driving from one side of Australia to the other, across the Nullarbor Plain included utilising a pair of stockings as a fan belt.

Determination and resourcefulness were a constant underlying theme in her life. A road trip to Charters Towers in Far North Queensland to go mustering had her brimming with pride in such an achievement. Training horses was a real passion and included providing horses for the film industry and being successful in the Victorian Quarter Horse Championships. This is a woman, who, when moving furniture while relocating house from "city" to "country" with just her 12-year-old daughter became challenging, came up with the motto "If a man can do it, we can do it!" It worked for us every time, guaranteed.

Calling my dad, that was the most difficult of all. I had not had contact with that side of the family for a few years. Mum insisted I return for visits with Dad when I went to live with her, however it was a 'pick one side or the other' family scenario and by choosing to live with Mum at age 12, that was apparently my decision made. After three subsequent visits to Dad and his family ended in tears, I did not return. It was clearly and painfully apparent I did not belong. Trying to think of what to say, I questioned whether I should even be notifying him. Did he deserve to know? Would he even care? I concluded that it was not my decision to make as to whether he attended the funeral or not. My responsibility was to inform of the facts and the responsibility of attendance and further family notification rested firmly with him. I did not possess the energy for diplomacy.

When Dad answered all I could muster was, "Mum's dead and the funeral is on the 24th" to which he replied, "Do you want me there?" It had not occurred to me that he would offer to be there for me. I had mustered the courage to call to notify, not to make more decisions. The added responsibility he had just thrust upon me, angered me. "I don't know! You were married to her, you have two sons with her, you all have a right to know, and you can choose whether to be there or not!" was all I could respond with.

On the day of the funeral, I was an emotional wreck. A lack of sleep and pure exhaustion meant I could barely retain enough energy to stay upright. I had cried, intensely, all morning. The funeral had been arranged and I had attended to the responsibilities it required but it all felt inadequate. I was angered by the fact that the only decision I was sure of was cremation. The attendees, all sorry for my loss, provided no comfort. Each well-wishing attendee was a step closer to my mother's finality. I felt guilty that I could barely respond to their condolences. Conversations were abound regarding "Carol's strength". Every person that knew my mother was impressed by her core strength, her determination, and her

The Funeral

infectious laugh. Hearing the stories of these mostly strangers recalling memories highlighting courage, cheekiness and ambition were of no comfort.

Then, I saw my dad. He came. One of only a handful of familiar faces in the crowd. An unexpected small feeling of relief came over me. Our eyes locked. The compassion in my dad's eyes was overwhelming and not something I had ever experienced. In that moment, albeit brief, my dad could feel my pain and it reflected clearly in his eyes. In that fleeting moment, I felt a fatherly care I had never experienced from my dad. My "Thank you for coming" was accepted with a hug of my hand and a response of "I thought I should". With his wife by his side, he retreated into the crowd. The short-lived relief was replaced by an intense loneliness. Her sons, for their own reasons, had chosen not to attend.

The open casket. Seriously, what is the right decision? Is there one?

Do I want people looking at me when I am dead? I do not know. Will an open casket give people an opportunity to say their goodbye? If I chose no to the open casket, would I be taking away this opportunity for others? I did not know! There were no physical deformities but her once glowing skin was now a ghastly orange. I had been informed that makeup would be applied so her orange skin would not be noticeable. I opted for the one that provided those that knew her with a final opportunity to say their private goodbyes during the "viewing". I did not feel I had the right to begrudge those who knew her this opportunity.

Upon entering the viewing area on my own, a flash of intense anger swept over me. Making my way to the casket I was determined to give her a piece of my mind. You promised me! How dare you! I do not want to be here! You had a choice, now I don't! If you were here right now, I would kick your arse! Then a wash of guilt flooded through my body. I am sorry Mum, but you deserve it. My anger at her quickly turned to an anger toward myself. Looking at her, I was painfully aware of a detail my mother would not have overlooked – her makeup!

Having brown eyes, Mum always insisted the only correct shades of eyeshadows were green, being her favourite, blue being the secondary option and browns used mostly for shading or enhancement. Subtle and natural looking – ALWAYS! The embalmers had used pink! A colour my mother would….arghhh not have been seen dead wearing! Mum insisted wearing pink eye shadow was not endearing and made her look like she had been crying. It was never worn by her. How could I have overlooked something which would be so important to her? This was knowledge I had within the first months of living with her. Now I had failed and she had been presented with a choice of makeup that she would hate. I am so sorry Mum.

Automatically I reached into the casket to hold her hand. The unexpected coldness of her body sent shockwaves

The Funeral

through me. Her warmth and her smile were gone forever. I had presented her to the world for the last time in bright pink makeup she would find just as ghastly as the horrible orange skin the terrible makeup was covering. I could not redo it, I could not rectify it. It was done, it was disgusting, and it was final!

The pain of this error became even more apparent when her sister walked to the casket to say goodbye. It was a hesitant gesture. Her sister was having difficulty deciding if she wanted to view the body at all. Walking out of the doors of the viewing area her angry words cut through me like a double-edged sword. "That is not my sister! It looks nothing like her! Who put her in pink makeup? Her hair is not even done! I wish I'd never seen it." All I could respond with was, "I know, I'm sorry".

The funeral service had only just begun and my lack of knowledge and foresight was again rising to the surface rapidly. I sat through the service, staring at the wooden casket, that I had selected, mostly based on price. The silver handles catching the light throughout the service were a painful reminder that Mum would not have cared about the box or the handles, but she *would* have been mortified by her pink makeup. How did I miss such a crucial detail?

Within weeks of the funeral, the inevitable news of my fiancé's mother passing arrived. The weight of death was too much to bear. Feeling like the worst person on earth, I ended the relationship. I did not have the emotional resources to support myself and most certainly did not feel it possible to support another's grief.

I was on my own with no one to turn to. I had not yet mustered the courage to go through Mum's belongings. I called my mum's widower to see if I could stay at the house until I went through her stuff and managed to sort myself going forward, to which he agreed. According to him, my mother would expect no less of him than to help me out.

I called my boss to let him know that I could not come back to work. I did not have a license and did not have a permanent home. My only option for immediate accommodation was two hours away. I was exhausted and barely able to function. Effectively, my life stopped.

SECTION 2

A Little of My Experience

Life With Dad

The earliest, most vivid memory I have, is of my mother leaving the family home. My mustard coloured, silk-edged "security" blanket tucked under my arm, thumb in mouth, wailing for my mum to come back. I watched the black Ford speed into the darkness down the driveway and out of sight. It was the end of my parent's marital relationship and any chance of amicability between them. I knew she was gone. I did not know why. I was three years old.

Within a short time, my dad received assistance from my mum's cousin. Once, early in the relationship, she left after being angered by my dad's behaviour after he had consumed alcohol at one of the private dance parties which they infrequently hosted. My father was visibly devastated. After locating her at a nearby caravan park, Dad made us dress in our best clothes and sat us in the lounge. We were going to visit her, and our job was made very clear; we were to be on our best behaviour, promise to be good, tell her we love her, and that we needed her. Dad was going to be doing the same and promise to never drink again. We did as we were told and Dad's pleas for her to return were successful. I never saw Dad drink alcohol again. She consequently became his second wife and stepmother to me and two older brothers.

By all accounts it was a supportive and successful marriage. On their wedding day, lined up with my two older brothers, we were asked one by one, from the eldest, what we would be calling my dad's new wife. It was presented to us that we had the option to call her by her name or to call her Mum. I was confused that this was a question. We already had a mum, and I did not want to answer. My two brothers had answered "Mum". I was not old enough or brave enough to provide a different answer. They always seemed to know the right thing to say.

Without a doubt my dad worshipped the ground my stepmother walked on. He was a committed husband, a hard worker and determined provider. This side of "my family", when you include them as a combined unit, is large and relationally complicated mostly due to death and divorce or relationship breakdowns.

In early childhood it was made brutally apparent just how alike I was to my mum, Carol. I was told repeatedly how I would "grow up to be a slut just like your mother". It felt like I should be ashamed of such an identity. Initially, I had

Life With Dad

no idea of the definition of a slut, and I was confused as to why it was so disgusting to be "like (my) mother". The bitter custody and access battle left its scars scattered throughout the family. There were sporadic visitations with Mum over the following years that always felt like a tug of war. As a child, there was an overwhelming feeling of guilt with each visitation accomplished. It was apparent, even to a child, that you were the reason for any continuance of a bitter relationship that was preferred to be forgotten.

Life with Dad was not all bad. There were times of fun, in particular their family functions where I was able to interact with people in more of my own identity and visiting Dad's clients as a family when he was working on their horses. I was able to enjoy playing with the other kids and for a while, identify as a normal part of a normal family. Life growing up consisted of horses and everything to do with a life that predominantly centred around them and travelling the local rodeo circuit. My siblings and I were riding horses before we could walk. A bit rough, a little tough with a hefty share of physical and corporal punishment but the overall concept of a predominately country and animal focussed lifestyle was good for any kid that liked a hint of adventure and had a love of animals.

My proudest Dad moment was at a rodeo. I was sitting on a hill overlooking the arena. I was allowed more freedom when travelling on the circuit so roaming the grounds was normal. The roping event was on, one of Dad's events. As I was opening the wrapper of an ice-cream, some creepy guy came around from behind a nearby truck. He grabbed my arm; the ice-cream fell to the dirt and he tried to drag me away from the arena. I screamed out in both pain from his grasp and the shock of the situation. Being regulars on the circuit, other rodeo regulars were easy to recognise, and I had not seen this stranger before. I screamed again and it got the attention of people nearby. The "rodeo-family" are quite a protective, family friendly bunch of people. Within minutes, the attention of what felt like the entire rodeo had surrounded us. I was scared, mortified and embarrassed. News must have shot around to the chutes where Dad was about to go out on his run. My dad, on his horse, came through the crowd. I was terrified of being in trouble for the scene created. Dad dismounted and I tried to quickly get out what happened. I was grateful to have the support of those that initially heard my screams. He was furious and the backing of the crowd was obvious. The guy was rapidly escorted from the rodeo and as they say, the show went on.

My dad had stood up for me. My dad had just protected me. Even when my stepmother scolded me for putting myself in such a position, I could not help but feel so proud that my dad had just come to my defence. I did not care how or why, just that he did.

I fondly recall his employment with a trucking company. A couple of times I had accompanied him to work, for whatever the reason and I did enjoy those one-on-one Dad-daughter moments. The company also had large Christmas functions with family-orientated activities, so we got to do activities together such as three-legged races. Laughing with Dad was infrequent therefore memorable.

My favourite "tough love" memory involved his occupation of breaking in horses. All three of us assisted with the numerous horses he worked with. My dad implemented the saying "if you fall off the horse, you get straight back on" literally. Forget your tears, your pain or anything else for that matter, get back on the horse. The only exception was if you had to go to hospital as one of my brothers had to when his leg was ripped open to the bone from a barbed wire fence while riding.

Dad had been working with a Shetland pony for a while and it was time for it to have a rider on its back. I was the appropriate fit for the horse so by default it was my job. The round yard we worked in was built of large round pinewood poles. There were tyres in between the top and bottom rungs for leg protection, being a standard round yard fit out. Everything was going well; I had mounted without incident and as usual we started off with Dad in the centre holding the tether going around the yard. As we progressed, Dad took the tether off the horse. Realising he was released and could fit under the bottom rung, the pony decided to go under the round yard rail with me on its back. I got knocked off by my chin and was scraped my entire front from the knees to my chin. I felt severely bruised and was sure I had broken ribs. "Get up and get back on the horse!" That was my dad in teaching mode, no time to be a princess. Although he was an excellent teacher and horseman, he was tough and especially in the early days, expected the same from his children.

It was around this time that my dad accidently reversed over me while I was in the driveway. This was another one of those ironic "don't be a princess" moments. Dad loved his panel van and to me, it seemed he was more concerned with possible damage to the car than to me. A couple of years later, I was struck by a vehicle on the way to school. I was under strict instruction to stay with my brother. He had insisted crossing the road before the school crossing. I was tangled in the front of the car and my brother had to run home to get my stepmother. Bursting in the door panicked, he announced comically "Jodi's been hit by a car!" Admittedly, his description of the events and how they unfolded were initially quite hilarious and I found the entire event just as funny as the rest of the family. However, it became an often-used taunt by both of my brothers to "go play on the road, hopefully third time lucky". This line became a source of amusement and joking. I, however found it hurtful, cruel and a constant validation that I was not wanted.

I was often confused by my brothers. They were always kinder when no-one was around, still brutish big brothers but kinder somehow. The moment another person entered, their demeanour toward me would instantly change, as if they were expected to show their hatred.

Life With Dad

My brothers' lack of sisterly love was appallingly apparent in high school. I was used to starting different schools as we had moved regularly during my primary school years. At one of those schools I had to embarrassingly try to explain re-attending after only previously being enrolled for three days. On my first day of high school, I was warned that I already had reason to watch my back. To no surprise, my brothers were in the elite school bully group and being their sister, I was an automatic target for their victims' retaliation. It was an intimidating start. It did not matter that unlike the other bullies' siblings I did not have the protection of my brothers. It made me an easier target. Any fear had to be quickly turned to bravado in my attempt to appear tough enough to conquer the path my brothers had laid before I was even at the gate. Few students seemed to match the strength or skill of my brothers, so I was able to use that knowledge as a hidden advantage.

Ironically, my closest ally during life with Dad, was my stepmother's mum, Nana. She had remarried after divorcing my mum's father's brother. A tough and resilient woman with a practical mindset and mischievous personality. I could be more relaxed in her company. There was a kind, yet forward honesty that came with her advice. Her role seemed to be that of the family confidante, that one everyone went to when they did not know where to turn to. The least judgmental and grudge-bearing. In my memory she was the most nurturing of the family and often provided a place to stay for those in need, including us.

During one such stay, she had accepted care of a neglected infant. The baby's skin folds were literally stuck together by dirt, including her tiny ears stuck to her small head. The baby had been abandoned by her mother and left with her elderly grandmother. Physically, the grandmother was unable to care for the infant even with the best of intentions and all the love in her heart. It was impossible to hold back tears during the numerous bathing sessions to gradually loosen the dirt. Nana loved the child back to health. I felt lucky to have not been as neglected as this baby had been. I wondered if her mother thought about her.

There was an 18-year-old girl who sought Nana's help who sadly, became a huge source of heartache for Nana. Experiencing some trouble at home, she came to stay with us. It was nice to have a younger girl around; it sort of felt like an older cousin staying with us. She was a very funny girl, and it was her who informed me of the meaning of the term "slut". One day she left to go into town and never returned. She was reported missing. Sometime later her body was discovered. Herself and some other women had fallen victim to a serial killer. It was my first experience of human death and the impact on Nana was excruciating to watch, feel and hear. Unexpected death, I learned, can be debilitatingly painful.

It was Nana who explained that my likeness in looks to my mum, meant that for some, looking at me was a constant reminder of a time people did not want to remember.

Life With Dad

Although it did not feel any fairer, I did get comfort from the fact that someone understood my inescapable burden.

There had been zero contact with my mum for a couple of years. Around 11 years of age, I had taken on my own secret initiative of trying to find my mum after being forcefully violated by strangers. Confused, in pain, ashamed and unable to confide in anyone, I felt disgusting, worthless, isolated and completely alone. Nauseated, I rejected the call to eat dinner. Money had been spent on Chinese take-away and my lack of appreciation of the provisions was met by being dragged up the hallway by my hair, to the dining table and firmly placed in the chair by my stepmother. The seat intensified my pain. Seeing the usual smirk on the face of my brother across the table stole my silence.

"Fuck you," I hissed much louder than I intended. "Why are you only nice to me when no one is around?" The words were followed by instant regret. My brother was visibly angered by my statement and swearing was a behaviour deemed fit for punishment. I was grateful to receive a mouth washing of soap and the wooden spoon to the hands. I had been dreading receiving the leather strap which would have forced my injuries and my secret to be exposed. The thought of revealing to my dad that others saw me just as he did, was terrifying.

Ironically and without further communication that same brother began avoiding me. He no longer pressured me to recreate the scenes of the book he had found in my dad's bedside drawer.

I desperately craved a relationship with my mum. Silenced by my surrounds I was unable to voice this to anyone. I felt weak, ashamed, confused and worthless. Where was my mum? Didn't she miss me? Why didn't she want me? Why couldn't I just get with the new family program like everyone else? I tried to understand how my brothers could not feel the same void in their hearts. They believed the venomous outpouring and at a young age, had aligned themselves with his hatred and condemnation of our mother.

My brothers were willing and able to cast her existence from their lives permanently. My attempts to ignore her memory and deny her existence were unsuccessful. I was living proof and a constant reminder of our mother's existence. It was burdensome, being cast as mini-Carol.

When I got "caught" smoking, in addition to being made to smoke numerous cigarettes and cigars, the usual corporal punishment was endured. There were, however, stark differences in standards of punishable behaviour for my brothers and I. They were boys, raised with an expectation to display some brutish, tough behaviour. Being the girl, I had the additional humiliation of lifting my skirt and/or pulling down my pants and bracing over the side of the bed when the leather strap had been selected. It was compulsory to count the lashings out loud. Losing count meant starting again.

Life With Dad

It was at this time the words escaped me. "I want to live with my Mum!" The words coming out of my mouth had the impact of a bomb. The shock on my dad's face was quickly replaced with the familiar look of angry hatred. Contact was made with an ex-partner of my mum, to request contact to see if she would be accepting of me moving in with her.

Immediately following the phone call advising my mum would accept me, I was handed a black garbage bag and told to fill it with clothes so I could be delivered to my mother.

I was confused as to how they could all hate me so much yet condemn me for wanting to be with my mum. The family had grown. They had conceived two girls and a boy. Rather than being an intrusion their presence in the family had a positive, stabilising effect. My stepmum seemed to take this opportunity to have a more settled down lifestyle, which my dad of course worked hard to accommodate. I was heavily included in my stepsibling's infant/toddler care and the bond between my stepmother and her children was easy to identify. I wondered if I would ever get to experience the joys of such a special bond. There was a slight softening to her personality with their births. I could see the connection between mother and daughters, that simply did not exist in the relationship between myself and her. I felt guilty I could not be what she needed for a daughter in the way my brothers had managed to fulfil being her sons. The son produced was no less than a special mini-Dad, obvious from the moment of his premature birth and adored by all of us.

I longed to have a large family one day, to have the bond they all seemed to share.

The memory of my father turning his head away from my intended kiss goodbye is painful. He was openly disgusted by my decision, wanted nothing more to do with me and he was angry. The scathing looks from my stepmother and my brothers were intimidating. It was obvious I had committed treason, and that was unforgivable.

I really had not expected to be listened to. I most certainly had not imagined to be on the way to my mum's house the very same day. On the short, tense, silent drive over, my heart was beating so hard I could feel it in my head. What had I done? Excited but scared, so many questions raced through my head. Did she want me, or did they make her accept me? Would she like me? Did I have Dad bits? Would she hate me for them?

After a short drive to the opposite side of town to where I had been searching, I was promptly discarded at the end of my mum's driveway, bag of clothes in hand.

I was 12 years old.

Life With Mum

There she was, standing at the front door, nervously waiting for my arrival. My bag of hand-me-down tomboy clothes thrown to the ground, I ran into her arms and cried with relief, hoping this was where I was meant to be.

During the phone call, she had been advised I had been caught smoking. Once we had composed ourselves and in preparation for a long night ahead, we walked to the shop across the road to buy cigarettes for me, during which she informed me she would be taking me to the Cancer Council to show me the effects of smoking. Although she smoked, she did not want me to and wanted me to be informed of the effects of the habit. I knew from this moment, my mum's style of education and teaching differed greatly from dad's.

We made our way into her loungeroom. "Are you a slut?" The words fell out of my mouth unintentionally. The shock on her face made me feel guilty instantly. Anticipating this was going to be a difficult process had not prepared her for my eager forthrightness.

During that first night, I learned that like me, my mum was the "less favoured child" in her family. We had scars on our chin that were disturbingly similar: "all men are bastards". Neither of us ever expected to be sitting there together, the person described to each of us did not appear to be the people we were meeting and the new living arrangements were going to take some adapting to for both of us. There would be no corporal/physical punishment. The first and most important thing on the agenda was that after living on her own for such a long time, my mum was used to her space to wake up in the morning. As a result, there was a strict no talking before she has finished her cup of tea. An easy rule – I had already mastered the art of silence.

My mum informed me that she did not know "how to be a mum to a 12-year-old," that we would have to "work it out as we go" and "be understanding of each other as we learn". I agreed to the ground rules without hesitation. I would have agreed to anything she stated. I was eager to belong, keen to adapt to her way of life and terrified of upsetting this unexpected but longed for opportunity.

I had not considered any ramifications of living with my mum. My arrival coincided with the purchase of her first home, in the country. Within a couple of months, we would

Life With Mum

be relocating. Shortly thereafter, Mum informed me I had an older sister that had been placed up for adoption prior to her relationship with my father. The process of locating the adopted daughter had been started many months prior and she was concerned about the impact of this new discovery and relationships going forward. Without hesitation I let her know I was receptive to the idea of an older sister and would happily support her regardless of the outcome. I felt like I had everything to gain and nothing to lose. Life was changing at a very rapid pace.

The hatred from my brothers and the anger triggered by my treason was humiliatingly and publicly displayed at my first ever social outing shortly after the move. I was permitted to attend the local Blue Light Disco. This felt like instant freedom. My father would not allow me past the letterbox of the driveway, so this was exhilarating and exciting. Within an hour of arriving, I was being warned by attendees that my brothers were looking for me. Their standing in the school community was that of a tough reputation that preceded their presence, and a barrage of warnings were coming my way.

"They're on the hunt for you and they don't look happy."

"I'd get out of here if I were you."

My excitement was quickly replaced with fear. Hiding in the shoulders of the crowd in my effort to not to be discovered,

I could see the determined anger on their face as they made their way through the crowd. I escaped out the front as they made their way to the back of the venue and phoned Mum to come and get me. We decided then as we were moving soon anyway, that it was probably a good idea to finish up at school the following day. I was grateful to be moving away.

Once we moved Mum enforced weekend visits with Dad. Although I protested, she was adamant that she would not keep me from Dad as he had done to her. I attended three visits. All ended in tears and nightmares. It was obvious that the anger was not dissipating with time as she had been expecting and the visits were creating further anger and causing distress. After thanking me for my co-operation and bravery, Mum informed me the visits were no longer mandatory. I did not return, Dad never phoned, and contact with any relatives ceased immediately.

It felt strange that my entire childhood just seemed to disappear. I was happy that I had an opportunity to belong, keen to learn and exist but it was sad and confusing that my life before Mum felt more like a bad dream from which I had been born. Just waking up after not hearing the alarm, starting further back than where I should be.

It was immediately apparent to my mum that I had not had the opportunity to harness nor was I encouraged to embrace my femininity. The manners learned during my time with Dad were not sufficient. It was important to my

Life With Mum

mum that I was able to adapt to different social settings; country manners were not enough in a 5-star restaurant. Her associates were people from various walks of life that included the hierarchy of bikie gangs, business owners, actors, actresses, elite national and international movie producers, tv personalities, sporting stars and billionaires. Life had taught my mum that you never knew who you might find yourself amongst so to avoid any potential embarrassment, she provided etiquette lessons at home. This extended to many fine dining establishments to include the selection, ordering protocol and responsible consumption of wine with the appropriate corresponding meal. I admired her ability to be equally at ease digging dirt or hosting a function for the elite.

When she was satisfied that I was able to navigate myself through elaborate social settings it was time to address my presentation. A visit to the dentist confirmed her suspicion that I required braces and an operation to correct the placement of my jaw. The additional expense of my arrival was becoming apparent, and Mum started to work nights in an effort to accommodate what she deemed as necessary requirements.

Feeling uneasy leaving her daughter at home alone while working at night meant that I was required to learn how to use her shotgun. Hoping I would never be required to use it, the knowledge of my competency provided her with the comfort that I was able to protect myself should dire circumstances occur without her present. We were both grateful of this foresight when one night I did have to shoot at an intruder. Consequently, we learned there was a "peeping-tom" doing the rounds around town.

Enrolment into a modelling and deportment school was to ensure I could get a rapid education on the basics of what she deemed to be acceptable social and formal presentation.

Life with Mum seemed to be a never-ending quest of education in life skills, versatility, adaptability and determination. Common sense, logic and independence were skills my mum had extremely high regard for and my demonstration of capability in these areas, often at crucial times, were proud moments.

On one such occasion, even I was surprised at the level of skill I had unwittingly acquired. One of her hobbies included that of beekeeper. Throughout her time of keeping and tending to the hives she had been stung on many occasions, but was not allergic and any reaction to the sting was minimal at worst. Hearing a banging at the front door, I walked out to find my mum lying on the steps, gasping for air, unable to speak more than a whisper, with her entire body swelling up and rapidly taking on the appearance of a mini sumo wrestler. Without thought, I dragged her into her car and drove her to the hospital in town. I had not been taught how to drive a car however I had learned to become an observant child and often intently watched

Life With Mum

my mum carry out seemingly menial tasks. The medical staff congratulated me on my actions, assuring me I had literally saved her life. A sting to the crown of her head had instigated an immediate allergic reaction. When she had recovered, she praised my ability to stay calm and in control throughout the situation and was mightily impressed with my unexpected driving skills.

A short time later, when it was discovered that she needed to have a kidney removed and was going to be hospitalised in the city for an extended period, she was concerned at leaving me to live on my own. We did not have a family or friend support system and were still quite new to the country town. Placing her faith in my assurances and without alternative options available, we agreed that I would make a determined effort to run the household, tend to the animals and ensure my schooling was not neglected. Missing the school bus was not an option; school was an hour and a half away, with no other access to public transport. Any absence would need to be explained and would possibly expose that at 14 years old I had been left without adult supervision and would be reported to the authorities. On her return from hospital, she was proud that I had exceeded her expectations, maintained the house, property and animals, fulfilled my schooling commitments and filled the freezer with pre-cooked meals to alleviate her of the responsibility of cooking on her return. Her tears of joy and gratitude had my heart pounding with pride. For me, failure had not been an option.

Many circumstances presented themselves that often had me taking on responsibility that far exceeded my physical age. I had proven to myself and my mum without doubt that even in dire circumstances I possessed a maturity that could be relied upon. So, when our property, animals and home were under threat from a bushfire it was once again time to step up. Trying to move the horses out of the direct path of the fire proved to be difficult. My horse had been rescued from the Ash Wednesday fires a couple of years earlier and the smoke of the fire had him panicked and terrified. Although he had ripped his leg open on the fence, his injury had to be ignored while I struggled to move them to more open ground where they had an improved chance of escape. On my return to the property Mum instructed me to put on the woollen clothing that we had made when she had taken on the task of teaching me to knit and placed me in charge of the water pump at the front of the property while she manned the larger pump at the rear of the house. We were unable to save a shed and greenhouse and the fences were destroyed. We had managed to maintain a small unburnt barrier around the home and our animals were safe. Exhausted, blackened by smoke, we celebrated. We had done it! Together, we had saved our home. In that moment I was convinced, no matter what this world could throw at us, together, we could overcome anything.

My mum had become my hero and my hero believed in me.

The Sister

Mum was about to meet her first born child. The anticipation in the car was palpable. I had not seen this side of my Mum; she seemed so unsure of herself. Fearful of the potential rejection and possible anger from the child she had placed for adoption nearly two decades ago.

Although I was nervous, learning that I had another sibling had been exciting and I was very eager to meet my big sister. We were not religious and for me, it felt strange to be meeting at a church, however we understood that if this were her support base it made sense that it would also be her most comfortable meeting ground.

There is a strong visual similarity amongst the women in our genetic line, so I had a preconceived idea of what my big sister was going to look like. Scanning the crowd before getting out of the car, I could not identify anyone that looked remotely similar and wondered if perhaps she had changed her mind and opted not to meet us. It was one of the many possibilities we had discussed on the drive.

As we approached the church, many of the congregation turned to observe us. It was obvious our arrival was expected. An elderly couple stepped forward to confirm my mother's identity and behind them was a large, anxious, red-haired girl – my new older sister. The long-awaited moment of meeting my big sister was here and appearing before us was the opposite of everything I had imagined. I scanned her person for any physical similarity to confirm our relation and I was disappointed that there were none.

The meeting went reasonably well. My older sister seemed just as eager as we were to explore this new family relationship and its potential. It was agreed that she would come to stay with us for the coming weekend, providing time and space to get to know each other and ask the inevitable questions that lingered unanswered.

During the initial meeting, we had learned that she had experienced much difficulty in her adoptive home and life. Most of her teenage years were spent in cycles of attending church to severe drug abuse, rehabilitation and back to church. By her own admission she did not know which lifestyle she wanted. Although she had recently completed time in a rehabilitation facility, she admitted to consuming alcohol regularly but denied currently using recreational drugs.

The Sister

The drive home was more relaxed. Mum was relieved and looking forward to the weekend. We were determined to make her feel comfortable and welcomed. In voicing my shock at her differing appearance, my mum simply replied, "And who are we to judge someone on their appearance baby girl? How about we get to know her?" She was right of course. Hadn't I loathed being judged for my appearance growing up? I felt ashamed that I had just placed that same judgement onto her because, at least physically, she appeared like her biological father.

Mum collected her daughter from the train station around lunchtime and we spent the afternoon exploring around town. The conversation stayed as general banter and we were all in good spirits. Mum prepared dinner and encouraged us to go spend time together while she tended to the needs of the animals. My sister said she liked being in the country and was glad she had agreed to meet with us.

After dinner came the inevitable big talk. Mum encouraged her to ask every question she had and said that she would do her best to provide any information that she felt she needed. The tragic circumstances around her adoption and her father's death were discussed at length. The adoption had been forced onto my mum by her parents and my sister learned that although her parents had been young, she had been a wanted child.

My sister assured Mum that she understood and accepted the circumstances of her adoption, that there was no need for Mum to feel guilt or regret and that she was thankful to now have contact. Admitting that she had always wondered if she had been a mistake and not wanted, learning that she had been adopted due to tragic circumstances after her birth had been a relief and having Mum search for her, provided a comfort that she had been longing for whilst growing up.

There were tears. There was laughter. There were hugs. We went to bed in the early hours of the morning, exhausted.

The following morning, Mum was up early and had cooked breakfast. Visibly happy with a beaming smile, she asked me to go and wake my sister. My knocks on the door were met with silence, so I opened it. My sister was slumped awkwardly halfway on/off the bed, her hair covering her face. I pushed her in an attempt to wake her causing her to fall to the floor, which took my attention to the empty pill containers. I screamed out to Mum.

Appearing at the door, the colour instantly drained from my mum's face. The joy I had just witnessed one minute ago had vanished. Without hesitation, Mum went into first aid mode.

My sister had attempted suicide.

Being in the country, it would take too long for an ambulance, so we struggled to drag her heavy frame to the car. Mum was taking her to the hospital and was adamant I was not

The Sister

going with them. I was to stay at home and Mum would be back whenever she could get home.

Watching them drive off, I was worried. Worried about my sister and confused. What about everything that you said just last night? I was desperately worried about my mum. This was worse than her worst fears which we had openly discussed. We had not discussed or prepared for this scenario.

Walking back into the bedroom, where I had just found her, my concern quickly turned to anger.

Why would you do this? Why now? How could you be so stupid? How dare you do this to our mother! My mum! You stupid, thoughtless, selfish, nasty person!

Picking up the pill containers intensified my anger as I realised this incident had been planned. While packing her bags, before arriving, before she had even taken an opportunity to get to know us, she had already planned for this moment.

As the hours passed, thoughts about how this would affect Mum tormented me. I was aware of how terrified she had been about this reunion and possible outcome. Aside from my sister dying, the outcome could not be more dire. What would this do to Mum?

Mum returned home once it was established that my sister would be ok. Visibly exhausted, she was not angry, she was sad and full of regret. Regret at the adoption, regret at the reunion, regret at exposing me to the confronting scene.

My 13-year-old brain wanted me to ask; what sort of person does this? How could she do this? Why would she do this? What makes a person even think about taking their own life?

The questions would not come out. I knew my mum would blame herself; she had already expressed her feelings of guilt and I could not bear to add to her pain by asking for explanations.

Almost two decades of wondering, an almost three-year search and within a week my mum had regained and again lost her eldest daughter.

It was the last I heard of or saw my sister.

A Friend & His Sister

My quest for early independence placed me in prime position for a party life. To quote a police detective at the time, I had entered a world where I was "a little girl, playing a dangerous game, in a big man's world".

This lifestyle, I know, hurt my mother deeply, although that had never been my intention. Her pain was apparent when she visited to let me know she would be moving back closer to the city. Making it clear that she would always be there if I needed her, she was unable to sit by and watch me slowly self-destruct.

In order to try to understand what was happening to me, she had visited a few therapists that had explained their understanding of my choices. Apparently, I was endeavouring to prove that I had an identity separate from my mother's. The years of being scathingly likened to my mother had turned me to try and stamp my own identity without dealing with the earlier abuse of my (predetermined) character.

With a teary cuddle she stated clearly, "I cannot watch you slowly kill yourself. If you ever decide to leave this lifestyle, please call me. I *will* be here. I *will* get you out. I promise."

It was some months later when real tragedy struck the group which I had surrounded myself with. This was a large eclectic group that consisted of varying ages, ethnicities and many interesting stories of some triumphs and many tragedies. It was a group where all were accepted, few were judged, and all could be forgotten in order to continue to party.

After a usual night of being out into the early morning hours a member of the group had returned home to find his sister's body hanging from the beams in the garage of the family home.

The experience changed my friend from a once cheeky personality into a withdrawn and vacant shell. The effect on the family dynamic was devastatingly apparent. Each member withdrew into their own grief and appeared unable to reconcile their anger or sadness in the aftermath. Guilt, blame and "what-ifs" plagued the family into decimation. Within mere weeks my friend attempted suicide in his wish to join his sister and escape the torture of discovering her body and the devastating aftermath.

A Friend & His Sister

It was his mother that discovered his attempt. His father successfully cut the rope and he was resuscitated by paramedics.

It was painfully apparent that the family dynamic had forever changed. Grief, blame, anger and sadness became a permanent blanket across the family.

In later discussions, my friend confessed that although he still had no desire to live, "where he went and what he saw" was a permanent deterrent to any future actual suicide attempt. The enormity of the impact he experienced was evident in the terror that spread across his face and a horror that could be seen in his eyes when speaking of the experience.

Although our familial history differed, the experience jolted the memories of discovering my sister's attempt. My mother's words just months previous began to haunt me. It occurred to me that although I was not deliberately "committing suicide" my mother was being forced to endure her daughter "slowly killing herself" and the guilt I felt was unbearable. I still had time to get my life on track before adulthood.

I made "that" call and true to her word, my mother was there. With support from both sides of the law, at opposite ends of the street, she kept her promise. My mum always fulfilled her promises.

Breaking the Cycle – My Way

After my mum's death and effectively stopping my life, it was her widower that helped me to re-enter life and begin working again. I was working hard. A full-time office position during the week, security at night and roofing on the weekends. I didn't socialise, I didn't make friends.

Eventually my own body decided to turn on me. What started with a normal menstrual cycle, one day just decided to not stop. The continual blood loss began to cause random fainting, not something my schedule could accommodate, especially during security shifts or whilst on top of a building on a construction site.

Dr K. had been my mum's doctor and consequently mine, immediately after I began living with her. He knew my story. I felt somewhat resentful that he knew some of my unknown in Mum's story. I guess I felt he possibly could have done more but she trusted him and had done for years before my time, so it seemed unfair to hold him remotely responsible. When questioned previously on his knowledge of her suicidal intentions he had responded with "I knew she was fragile". I'd been angered by his response.

According to western medicine, there was "no reason" for my permanent bleeding. Iron supplements were not enough to compete with the blood loss. A solution needed to be found and I was open to options. The quickest option presented itself in the form of an operation. A hysterectomy.

At 21 years of age, with no children, this option would leave me childless for life.

In order to proceed with the operation a session with a psychiatrist was required to ensure I fully understood the impact of the operation, being that I would be unable to conceive or carry a child for the rest of my life.

My mum's widower helped to prepare me for the psychiatrist by sharing his knowledge of the "psychology practices used" in these types of appointments. Justification had been rationalised and answers to the impending questions had been rehearsed prior to the scheduled appointment in order to ensure the operation would proceed:

Breaking the Cycle – My Way

Why would I want to bring a child into this bastard world?

Why would I knowingly bring a child into a world of hate, contempt, callous destruction and cruelty?

If I was so like my mother, what if I decided to suicide? Was I then not just repeating the cycle? Was I prepared to bring a child into the world potentially abandoning it, knowing the pain such an act could cause?

How could I knowingly bring a child into a world that allows it to be abandoned, unloved, unwanted and destroyed?

The impact on future romantic relationships? This one was simple – if a man only wants me for children, he doesn't really want me at all!

I was convinced that this operation was just going to ensure I was going to end the cycle of pain and permanently avoid a potential disaster – another unwanted child in a nasty, uncaring, cruel and lonely world. If I did not want to repeat the mistake of my parents, this operation provided a 100% irreversible guarantee.

The rehearsals had been a success. The psychiatrist had not been expecting me to be so "well-equipped" with the responses to his questioning and with an impressive psychological report, gave the approval for the operation. I would be childless for life.

The Pact

Without much thought of any meaningful future, when it was suggested to enter a suicide pact, I could not think of any reason not to. The pact partner had interrupted a previous suicide attempt of mine, was aware of my recent history and had anticipated my willing co-operation.

There were numerous conversations which centred mostly around leaving their loved ones behind. Although I questioned the pact partner's reasons and justifications, I was not in the frame of mind to convince them of anything or try to negate their justification. They were in a current unsuccessful custody battle and did not have access to their children.

Suicide for me now was not just an option, it was my destiny. I had never felt like I belonged in the world. Everyone seemed to have a connection, a place in the world. My only connection had gone. There was no-one for my suicide to affect and I had a newfound empathy and understanding around the decision my mum had made. I was indeed growing up to be "just like my mum". I had finally come to the realisation that my fate had been decided long ago and there was no point in fighting it.

After the deliberations, the planning and preparation for the event happened rapidly.

Fading off into unconsciousness in the passenger seat, the assistance of intoxication allowed me to float off with the hum of the V8 engine. My awareness of the presence of another human being had subsided.

Without warning a fist hit the side of my head from the driver seat and I was jolted back into consciousness. The presence when I opened my eyes could only be likened to that of an animal in instinctive survival mode. A violence that could not be tamed and had nowhere to go except straight for me. I scrambled to get away trying to overcome the effect of substance abuse and fumes.

Chased after, dragged by my hair and thrown to the ground, I fought back with my own instinctual ferocity, getting away and out the front door. The commotion had caught the attention of neighbours and the bloody sight of me had initiated their call to police.

The Pact

When the police arrived, I instinctively tried to alleviate any blame, however the person in question had run out the back door and over the fence. Unimpressed by my bloodied appearance and many excuses, they went on to search, find and deal with the person.

Released by the police, whatever unfolded that day between that person and the police was a topic that was forbidden to be discussed. I was however enlightened on my newfound burden of responsibility and ensuing guilt for being willing to participate in an event that would have caused pain to the pact partner's children.

On this day, I realised that suicide is not an option for all people and a suicide pact was no longer an option for me.

The Weapon

The first time my mother's suicide was used as a weapon, I was speechless.

It didn't matter that the perpetrator did not know my mum. The shock and hurt was palpable in my silence and the narcissist (who ironically, had been adopted out at birth by their own mother) that had delivered the callous remark smiled smugly, proudly observing the impact of their words as the blood drained from my face.

My frozen silence allowed the words to echo over and over in my head.

"At least your mother had the guts to kill herself, you can't even do that you fucking useless coward, she'd be ashamed of you."

This and many other callous remarks have been successfully utilised as weapons to manipulate, wound and control me. These statements compounded and continued my inner-anguish, pain, shame and propelled the self-disgust deep into my core. Many times, over many years.

"Ya father didn't want ya, ya mother couldn't hang around for ya and ya can't even give a man kids, see what fucking good are ya to anyone? Nuthin to no-one, go kill yaself, do everyone a favour, go on, do somethin' to make ya mum proud."

This was probably the most collectively brutal statement delivered to me and it was excruciatingly painful that I could not refute it because basically, the statement was a factually correct summation of my worthlessness. A mere verbalisation of what I already felt.

Other than feeding my already existing lack of self-worth, this statement often brought my anger to the surface.

Angry that the statement was correct, angry that I couldn't muster a worthy response, angry that my parents' loveless actions could be utilised as weapons of destruction to which I felt I had no defence. Angry that I was unloved and unlovable.

During my numerous moments of self-doubt, sabotage and destruction I eventually adopted this line to self-criticise,

The Weapon

helping to feed the shame of my existence and justify my lack of entitlement to a peaceful or fulfilling life.

The reality of these or similar statements is that they are a clear indicator of a toxic person/relationship. Merely another selection of words for maximum benefit of manipulation, degradation, and belittlement. A clear lack of compassion, understanding, empathy, consideration or accurate knowledge. A reflection of character to those that verbalise such statements and a clear indication of an individual that should be avoided, removed from your life and never given the opportunity to consume your energy or attention.

Interaction with and acceptance of this toxicity has been detrimental to my mental health.

My mother's memory is worthy of a more loving reflection and my energy is better spent in more productive and worthy relations with myself and others.

SECTION 3

Our Power As Humans

Common Obstacles

In my experience the most common obstacles I have witnessed in overcoming the mental health impacts of traumatic experiences are a necessity to allocate blame, the inevitable judgement and an inability to access a perspective of acceptance.

In the event of no answers or palpable reasons of a death by suicide, there remains permanent questions for those affected, which inevitably have many hypothetical possibilities that extend as far as the imagination will allow. The "What Ifs?" are immeasurable and can become their own constant never-ending source of torture.

For me, knowledge of the hardships my mother endured throughout her life made understanding her decision, or even more so her timing, more difficult. With a proven track record of overcoming seemingly insurmountable challenges, her determination had been unquestionable.

Seats of Suicide

Trying to find reasons and answers becomes a never-ending, tumultuous quest. There are no complete answers to the multitude of questions that constantly beg for attention. Often, answers found lead to more questions and the scope for questions just gets wider.

Finding one or more sources to blame does not end the inner turmoil and umpteen questions. It does, however, provide a funnel for anger and allows you to keep the gut-wrenching hole in your being. Although this keeps their presence alive, which is something we are desperate to hold onto, it is also instrumental in keeping your pain to a living, palpable and current issue, never put to rest.

Finding a particular person to be responsible for our loved one's suicide does not alleviate the pain, guilt, trauma, grief or close the gaping hole of emotions. Often, this "source" then becomes a target for a self-justified victimisation, more pain, anguish and, inevitably, frustration and anger, yet still the void remains. This focus becomes an obstacle in our ability to fully experience joy and negates the ability to experience inner peace.

In being exposed to suicide, we have also been exposed to various forms of destructive human behaviours, whether it be relational, physical and/or emotional. Witnessing domestic, parental, relational violence and acts of aggression toward ourselves/our loved ones can be psychologically damaging. So too can the effects of a lack of relational boundaries, support,

Common Obstacles

safety and nourishment (physical & emotional). When these instances take place in the perceived sanctuary of our home, they are confronting, disturbing and most often not explained. The consequences (unintended or otherwise) are left to unravel, slowly seeping into the overall consciousness of the home. The debrief required is not considered and the issue will not have been effectively dealt with. Each member of the household will interpret and incorporate the exposure according to the experience – or lack thereof – and knowledge of the individual at that time.

From this understanding, there is a collective blame able to be allocated to every human being. A necessity to understand that as a society there is collective inability/unwillingness to grasp the basic human concept of self-awareness, hence a lack of self-responsibility and a common perspective of limited power in our ability to determine the quality of our existence and consequential impact as an individual.

The perception of everything external to us being paramount as an ultimate power is common in the society of today and is crucial to the underlying success of the commercial world. We exist in a society that professes inclusion under a guise of segregation and has mastered diminishing the power of individuality through conformance to commonplace, yet ever-changing, acceptance and rejection values. The magnification and ever-increasing complexity of such a society dwarfs the perception of the necessity in understanding the power of our individual abilities, self-responsibilities and the application of such resources to ensure an environment that is imperative to, and supportive of, enhanced mental health fitness.

This model of society is enhancing an individual perception that worthiness is to be found outside of oneself. Searching for the validation of worthiness via external stimuli whether that be in your job, relationships, achievements, social or financial status is an assurance that your emotional and mental health fitness will flourish or deteriorate according to the inevitable fluctuations of all, or one, of these external gratifications. When one and/or all of these become difficult to manage or no longer exist the way we perceive they should, the emotional distress can become overwhelming and create a perception of failure with an inability to recover from the impact of the situation being experienced.

External situations, items and relationships are an opportunity to enhance our existence, they are not the entirety of our existence. Your responsibility, as part of your species is in your capacity as an individual to contribute to the overall longevity and strength of the species. The management of your interactions throughout your journey will determine your overall impact as a human to contribute to the strengthening or weakening of your environment, offspring, the society in which you function and the species. The human species is directly responsible for the environment into which we are born.

Common Obstacles

An inability to navigate and understand our emotions in the rawest form has contributed to a perspective of helplessness and a sense of entitlement, enhancing a lack of self-awareness and self-responsibility. An increased sense of entitlement leads to an enhanced sense of devastation and worthlessness when that perception of entitlement is challenged, diminished or negated.

It is inevitable that throughout a human existence, material possessions will come and go, relationships will start and end, lives will begin, and lives will end. There will be many beginnings that will have endings. There are numerous situations to be navigated and each situation will be partnered with emotions. The emotions and their intensity will vary greatly throughout the entire existence. These emotions include but are not limited to wonder, elation, anxiousness, confusion, humiliation, aggravation, intimidation, strength, weakness, embarrassment, joy, happiness, anger, relief, frustration, grief, sadness, sorrow, guilt, shame, numbness, exhaustion, pride, satisfaction, love, disgust, disappointment, overwhelm, dread, anticipation, regret and many more. In other words, you are human.

By choosing to learn to be consciously aware of our emotions, learning and accepting their messages of guidance and appropriately responding to the need identified, we open ourselves to the opportunity of consciously practising understanding, empathy, compassion and consideration when interacting with ourselves and others.

In practising understanding, empathy, compassion and consideration with those with whom we interact, we promote a wider supportive environment that encourages acceptance and equality. Your existence as an individual has an impact. In accepting conscious self-awareness and responsibility an individual can determine the quality of their familial, societal and generational impact.

The only true power we hold throughout our journey is within the management of ourselves. In order to effectively manage ourselves we need a greater understanding of the implications and consequences of our reactive emissions that have been enhanced by a sense of privileged entitlement.

When we believe we can justify our inappropriate reaction to another because of their actions we have at that time alleviated ourselves of the responsibility of self-awareness, negated an opportunity for growth and understanding, hindered our capacity to accept what is and ultimately surrendered to limiting our perception of choices. Our inability or unwillingness to accept what is, provides us with a justification of thoughtless and reactive behaviours. Thoughtless and reactive behaviours are perfect ingredients to create a journey of tumultuous mental health and an ever-challenging existence.

Our acceptance of self-awareness does not alleviate others of their responsibility. Self-awareness allows us to be mindful enough of our needs and the impact of our existence in order

Common Obstacles

to maximise the potential of a manageable and meaningful outcome. The mis/management of our actions in responding to each situation and encounter, is the determining factor in the manageability of the outcome.

When a conscious effort is applied to self-awareness, the ability to encounter situations, navigate appropriate relations and undertake practical steps of problem-solving without investing unnecessary emotional energy is heightened. This increases your ability to access, harness and maintain an inner peace conducive in creating an environment for stable mental health. This process allows a wider scope of perception for opportunities of relational growth and maintenance.

The Blame Game

In the quest to find someone to blame, I have found the trail is never-ending – or is it? In offering my life as an example, who could we blame?

The times I have been ready to commit suicide, there has of course been people around me. Some suggested that I was now predisposed to suicide because of my mother's suicide, some readily offered their reasons as to why I should, some actively encouraged me to undertake the act. A few tried to find a reason why I should not and endeavoured to provide some words of discouragement.

Some individuals' actions prior to a successful suicide would have been deemed not only abhorrent but also criminal. In the event of my death under these circumstances some blame would have put toward an abuser. In shedding light on a colourful and challenging life, the perpetration of violence against me would have been deemed as obvious justification for suicidal ideations, even without being the offspring of a suicidal parent.

When a perpetrator utilised my previous traumas as current acts of aggression, they were powerful, degrading, difficult to tolerate and justified my lack of self-worth. If I believe that I deserve to be treated better, why would I allow a person to repeatedly abuse me?

Without alleviating the responsibility of abusers, I would like to challenge the obvious allocation of blame.

If I had been successful in suicide, with accessible records providing irrefutable evidence of varied abuse, initial investigations would have placed blame on the perpetrator. It is likely that my mother and father would have been deemed partially responsible.

That would be the quickest and easiest place to lay the blame, however let us look a little deeper. A perpetrator of abuse is a broken human being. Angry, scared, confused, intimidated, worthless and frustrated are just some of the plethora of emotions at play during the abuse they spew at the world around them. The reasons for the abusive human are a by-product of their perception of the surroundings they have been exposed to. I refer to their perception, because two humans can experience the same event, however the perception and recollection of the event will vary with the individual perception and experience of the same event, including their unique personal feelings of the experience.

In cases of extreme medically diagnosed mental illness, responsibility for criminal actions ceases due to impaired mental faculties. In simplistic terms, you are held accountable to the degree of your mental "fitness" or psychological impairment.

In order to lay a justified blame at the feet of the perpetrator of the violence that "pushed me over the edge", would it not then only be fair to investigate further? Is it appropriate to lay the blame at a differently damaged human being? Where does the line stop? If you shift responsibility for one persons' action to another, then where does the line stop? In recognising that a perpetrator is also damaged, should it not then be further investigated to place blame for the damage done? Do you then blame the parents of each or one individual? If not the parents, as they provided resources and support as it was required, does it then pass to the grandparents or perhaps their great grandparents?

What about the therapy? Is it appropriate to lay blame with the therapist? What about the governments? In finding a multitude of possibilities and many unanswered questions, the blame is still not really allocated.

As an example, if an individual attends anger management therapy but is unable to alleviate the anger issues, who is to blame? The therapist? The teacher of the therapist? The education, resources, or lack thereof? Can blame be justified if the subject was unable to comprehend the complexities attached to the behaviour they have displayed in their quest for a self-meaningful existence?

Whose responsibility is it to teach each human the basic psychology of human behaviour?

With the benefit of hindsight, my life is disturbingly yet almost boringly predictable. The nature of my parents' relationship early in my childhood allowed the creation of a perception that I was powerless within relations and to my emotions. Emotion was to be endured and my power as an individual was minimalised. Effectively, life was to be endured. I highly doubt this was the intention of my parents when I was conceived or born.

Experiences and exposures after early trauma exacerbated that lack of identity and assisted a deeper perception of lack of worthiness. Any concept of self-acceptance, self-awareness and self-responsibility were void.

At various stages throughout life, we get to choose who we surround ourselves with. Those we are exposed to, domestically, socially and professionally all have a degree of impact on our mental and social fitness. Those we choose to surround ourselves with, are directly associated to our own values and self-worth.

The Blame Game

This being the case, if I have a perpetrator of abuse within my immediate circle and then further allowed them to remain despite their abhorrent abuse, is it not then relevant to ask what purpose they are serving in my life? Do I feel powerless within my own journey? Does my lack of self-worth require their abuse to justify the perception I have of myself and my place in the world? Is my desire to have others accept me at the expense of, or due to, my inability/unwillingness to accept myself or understand my behaviour and the associated emotional reactions?

This is not to condone abuse of any being, alleviate abusers of responsibility or victim blame, however if we take a step back from the abusive acts and provide an empathetic perception of the perpetrator as an individual person, we now have two individually damaged beings, fighting for a mostly sub-conscious, reactive type of survival. Individuals operating from a dominant sub-conscious realm of egotistical survival are functioning without the ability to locate the emotional determination for the behaviours displayed or experienced by the self. Any co-habitation becomes based on a sub-conscious co-dependence. The concepts of self-awareness or self-responsibility are void in existence.

If these two humans, that are now functioning from a predominately reactive sub-conscious based perspective, also pro-create, the offspring of the relationship are now further displaced from any concept of self-worthiness, self-acceptance, self-awareness or self-responsibility.

If we return to the parents, what were the experiences and exposure of the parents to create them as individuals? In identifying the grandparents, do we not have to ask the same question? And so on.

The blame game becomes a continuous cycle that quite frankly dooms every individual that has existed with some form of responsibility for the state of our current worldly mental health fitness.

If it can be judged that my parents could have provided me with a better experience, am I/those in judgement, now providing myself with a better experience? If I can judge that society could have been a better environment, am I contributing to society with that same knowledge? If I can judge that the last generation could have provided the current generation with a better worldly state, am I now contributing to the world as I have judged? What is the purpose of my judgement?

Am I consciously responding to the emotion that promotes the formation of my judgement or sub-consciously reacting to the feelings of my experience and exposures, without adhering to the same judgement?

At the point that we believe we can blame what was a right/wrong decision, justified/unjustified behaviour when utilising the benefit of hindsight, then so the opportunity presents itself, to practice a perception of acceptance, therefore a provision for education. This empowers us, as individuals, to navigate into the realm of self-acceptance.

Self-acceptance is empathetic in nature, void of judgement and an integral component in the quest for a journey of self-awareness and self-responsibility. In gaining a perception of self-acceptance we become empowered as individuals to actively respond to ourself and those we encounter on our journey in a manner that instigates the difference that we have identified.

The futile necessity of allocating blame becomes void with the application of a perception of empathy toward the complexity of each individual human journey, including our own. The importance of self-analysis, self-expression, self-awareness and self-responsibility of every individual becomes alarmingly apparent.

Acceptance is not forgiveness, an allocation of responsibility or condoning of behaviour.

"Acceptance in human psychology is a person's assent to the reality of a situation, recognizing a process or condition without attempting to change it or protest it." - Wikipedia

An inability or unwillingness to accept, hinders the ability to reconcile. An inability to reconcile, hinders the ability to identify and therefore adequately address an imbalance.

Blaming The Clouds Will Not Stop The Rain

We can however identify the clouds, the potential for rain and consciously choose to stand in it, getting drenched and possibly ill from the exposure we have allowed. Alternatively, we can choose to source an umbrella or move ourselves undercover, limiting the amount of exposure and consequential effects.

Judgement

Many years and an enormous amount of my energy has been consumed by overwhelming feelings of shame, guilt and a general sense of unworthiness. This has hindered my ability to perceive worthy options for myself, to experience joyous moments and created self-perceived restrictions on pursuing and achieving my dreams and desires. These feelings have resulted in limited positive social interaction, destructive personal relationships and behaviours, limiting my perception on the concept of freedom as an individual.

How did I make those choices? I should have….I could have….why didn't I….?

Some will say it is easy to see how my life unfolded as it did. There will be others that will find it difficult to comprehend some of my life events and consequent decisions. A few will condemn. Myself? With the benefit of hindsight, I can see why my life has been challenging.

It is easy to sit in judgement on past events however this judgement is unfair and unjust.

At any given moment, we function only with the knowledge and our perception at that moment. Within moments, hours, days, months and years inevitably, within the experience of life itself our knowledge increases, and our perception can be changed. The amount of increased knowledge and any change in perception will vary greatly.

The judgement passed on any recent past or historical decision, action or event now has the benefit of increased knowledge, a differing accessibility to resources and a vision of possibility that were not previously available. The facts now readily accessible were not available or were uniquely obscured from the person and the situation being experienced at that point in time.

If the information that is now accessible was available and considered with the same perspective now held, the selection process would have been varied, the option selected would likely have been different and the outcome would differ according to the variances now being considered. The opinion able to be formed in the present has the benefit of the addition of hindsight. Any experience, knowledge, sensation, information or overview now within consideration

Judgement

has irrefutably changed from the original selection criteria available, considered, accessed or processed.

The only unique aspect of our entire existence is our perspective. Our perspective is formed as a direct result of the knowledge obtained from our unique experience of, and varying depths of exposure to, the multitude of differing life situations and events.

It is these variances that now allow the cast of judgement to be thrown. Without the additional benefit of hindsight, the original decision is made.

In order to provide a clearer understanding of the above information I refer to the following analogy:

Take a child and place them in the centre of an art room. Give the child some paint and ask them to create a picture. Now leave the room.

When you re-enter the room, you are annoyed that the child has created a mess, painting by hand on the walls and proceed to reprimand the child for not using utensils to create their work of art.

You did place the child in the art room. The very nature of the title suggests that there are art supplies available; however, did the child know what supplies are contained in an art room? Did the child have prior knowledge of art utensils? Did the child know of the existence or the location of the paint brushes or paper? Were the paint brushes visible to this child? Were they accessible to this child? Were they permissible or deemed required in their understanding of the situation they were in?

Given this scenario, it is unjust and unfair to reprimand the child for not using paint brushes or paper. There was no consideration of using the brushes because the child, at that point in time was unaware of the possible existence or inclusion even though the brushes and paper were in the room. However, it is now far more likely that if you were to place the same child in the same situation, they will, at the very least, now consider the paint brushes and paper, allowing for a different choice. Their awareness of the situation with the benefit of hindsight has changed, not the situation itself.

It is important to note that this lesson does not now mean the child will automatically use the brushes and paper in future. If the child is bashful, they may be too shy to ask for the additional supplies. If the supplies are on a shelf the child may not have yet reached the height to access them. Placed in a cupboard, the child may not feel entitled to opening the cupboard to access the brushes. A hurt child may refuse to use the brushes altogether, resenting the unjust reprimand.

The introduction of knowledge and resources does not in itself alter the outcome. It does however offer possibilities to a range of outcomes. The perception of the knowledge

Judgement

presented and the understanding of accessibility and perception of benefit according to the individual considering the additional knowledge and resources will be the ultimate determining factor of the outcome.

In hindsight, I can see the reasonings of my younger self. I understand where her choices came from, however my present self cannot fathom repeating many choices given the same circumstances. In fact, the decisions would often be completely the opposite of the choices previously made. Put simply, that same perception and logic no longer exist. The personal strengths, resources, logic, perception of abilities are different. The relational, situational and self-awareness aspects of the self, have irrefutably changed.

Analysis of hindsight can ensure clearer foresight. However, in applying the burden of judgement, we also apply an unnecessary accumulation of guilt, shame and toxicity. This perspective hinders the ability to recognise or form a manageable concept of self-worthiness and self-acceptance. The inability to access this aspect of self-awareness consequently hinders the ability to self-regulate our responsibility to enforce crucial situational and relational boundaries.

Toxic Relations

The reasons used to justify or make sense of death by suicide include financial, educational, professional, social, health and in my experience, always include the topic of relationships.

Where a glimpse of suicide exists, so does a toxic relationship. This is true even for the socially isolated. The relationship with oneself has become a permanent heartache, experienced in a perception of failure and worthlessness with an emotional burden that appears inconceivable to bear.

Regardless of the justification applied in order to commit to the idea, threaten the intent or carry out the ordeal, the now dominant toxic relationship has been allowed to permeate and fester under the surface. For those that have not isolated themselves, the toxicity from the relationship with oneself will have also permeated the personal and social relationships in which you are involved. Many of these relationships will not, at least initially, have a toxic appearance.

When at the point of suicide, the strength of the emotional trauma endured is perceived as inescapable and is consumingly powerful. We have, albeit unwittingly, become our very worst enemy, armed with an incredible array of self-criticism and degradation intent on justifying our belief that although we do exist, we cannot, and we should not. A plethora of unaddressed emotions and a perception of weakness in the ability to navigate any form of existence has now become the dominant army in the battle for life. The perception of forces outside ourselves seem excruciatingly more important, powerful and dominant in our world than the pathetic and meagre existence now felt of oneself.

Likely, the toxic relationship with oneself will have commenced as a result of our environmental experiences and relationships. For many, this may have begun in early childhood before we were afforded the responsibility or possessed the ability to define our immediate environment for ourselves.

It is generally accepted that from birth others are responsible for our physical nourishment, maintenance and support. As we grow older, we are taught to feed ourselves according to the culinary skills of those that care for us. We learn the use of utensils and food variations such as vegetables being good, confectionary being bad. We rely on those responsible for us to keep us clean and clothed and ensure an environment in which we can sleep. As we grow into adulthood, most individuals instinctively accept the responsibility of tending to their physical nourishment, maintenance and support.

Once we have accepted the basic responsibility of physical nourishment, some of our earlier teachings and learned dietary intake requirements will be modified according to our individual taste, culinary discoveries and personal choice, regardless of our perception of the quality of physical nourishment provided to us when we were reliant on those responsible for us. As an example, if you were not taught to cook, you do not automatically accept that you will never be able to and therefore starve. Most people will seek, learn and acquire a means with which to provide themselves with some form of nourishment to sustain their physical survival.

Accepting the responsibility for your mental health fitness and maintenance is crucial, regardless of the quality of mental health care provided before you were afforded the responsibility.

Just as our physical appearance and functionality is directly dependant on the amount and quality of nourishment (food), maintenance (personal hygiene/physical activity) and support (sleep/safe environment), our mental health is reflected in and variable to our environmental and relational surrounds.

Seats of Suicide

A physical diet consisting of wants such as sugars and processed foods whilst neglecting the dietary needs of crucial vitamins and minerals will inevitably create physical ailments and/or affect physical abilities. Mental health fitness is no different. A diet that consists predominantly of nourishment to personal gratification and egotistical entitlement whilst neglecting any necessity of discipline, consideration or empathy, will be reflected in your environmental surrounds and directly impact the functionality of personal and societal relationships. These consequences will affect and be a determining factor that contribute greatly to your mental health fitness.

Humans have an instinctual need for connection and acceptance. It is what our survival as a species depends on. It is our perception of our role within and management – or lack thereof – of these connections that enhances or decreases our quality of life and directly impacts our mental health. It is our perception of the importance of each connection that is reflected in the personal relationships we choose to surround ourselves with. These choices are, in turn, reflected in life experience and exposure.

As an example, if our self-worth has become reliant on acceptance from others, the penalty can become a lack of self-acceptance.

When we continue to accept unacceptable behaviours, the behaviour itself will become deemed as acceptable. When we continue to tolerate intolerable situations, the situations will become deemed as tolerable.

Even with the intent of helping others, we can lose sight of the long-term consequences of our actions. Again, this is often not a conscious process. Helping others is a desirable, endearing, admirable human trait and an integral component in every community. The benefits to the giver and receiver are often immeasurable. However, in helping others, it is important to recognise when our help is in fact a hindrance, disguised.

When we help others despite themselves, we begin to alleviate them of their requirement for self-responsibility and hinder their perspective of self-awareness. In providing the same continuous "help" and accepting the consequences of repeated behaviours, we are negating others of the consequences of their decisions and behaviours. This then hinders the perception of the requirement for personal analysis, growth, education, change and can potentially obstruct access to more adequate resources.

We are no longer helping as we initially intended.

We can provide opportunity for growth, assistance in knowledge or different perspectives, promote resource assistance and support. We cannot successfully undertake the actions for someone without their balanced input, without also undermining the initial intention of the provision of assistance.

The quality of the connection we have with ourselves is reflected in the quality of our interactions and relations with others. The behaviours we choose to retain or reject for ourselves and from others, is a direct reflection of the degree of stability of our self-perception. This is the core function of boundary navigation, assertion, regulation and enforcement.

An inability to navigate boundary regulation, assertion and enforcement, hinders the ability to identify, establish, or maintain a perception of self-worthiness.

Any perception of unworthiness obscures the ability to identify, establish, create or maintain relations conscious of self-awareness and self-responsibility.

A lack of self-awareness and self-responsibility is conducive to an environment of destructive behaviours, reactive interactions and toxic relationships.

The Power of Perspective

The perspective we hold as individuals is predominantly a sub-conscious collaboration of our experiences, exposures and interactions that include the associated emotions attached to these events. In relying on our sub-conscious realm to dictate our perspective, we can allow the power of our perspective to be formed from a basis of our fears, insecurities and judgment.

When we apply a consciousness to our perspective, the awareness surrounding the influence on our decisions and abilities, including the potential power of our perspective, increases. The realms of possibility on our journey are limited only by the limitations exercised in this process.

The willingness to challenge our current held perspectives can be crucial in achieving what we previously deemed as unachievable, or overcoming a seemingly unsurmountable experience, situation or event.

Our perspective does not alter the situation or circumstances. The willingness to understand our perspective and the basis of the perspective we hold of ourselves and our environment can be a powerful tool for altering our current existence from unbearable to bearable, or to change a situation previously deemed unmanageable to manageable.

Our perspective can be the determiner in whether we live a life with purpose or a life of self-destruction. In fact, our perspective can literally be the difference between life and death.

Perspective is not necessarily right or wrong, it just is. For many years I held the perspective that "I was born for everybody's shit". This perspective allowed me to tolerate situations, exposures and circumstances many would deem as overwhelmingly intolerable.

When I first succumbed to wanting to take my own life, I was around 23 years old. Prior to this moment I had maintained a perspective that death by suicide was unacceptable. In getting to the point of trying to take my own life, suicide rapidly became an acceptable and welcomed alternative to the debilitating emotional pain and sheer exhaustion that I was enduring.

The Power of Perspective

It was the end of my first legally binding relationship. I had welcomed the end of the relationship to this person who was more than double my age, however the circumstances that I found myself in at the end of the entanglement were disturbing, excruciating and debilitating. The deliberate efforts of the other person were socially devastating, publicly humiliating, emotionally exhausting and at times cunningly dangerous and criminal.

Every single item including my toothbrush and clothing had been cleared out of the home we inhabited in mere hours and without warning, whilst I was at work. The only item left had been my fish tanks because they were unable to be placed into storage.

All bank accounts had been cleared out of funds. Despite a physical altercation, I managed to maintain possession of the keys to my car, which was under finance. Further actions taken against me included inaccurate yet grossly descriptive letters that were predominantly sexual in nature sent to every employer, including venue management and co-workers, school friends that I had not been in contact with for many years, family members that I was not in contact with, and any possible future associates. With efforts to reduce me back to previous addictions, large amounts of amphetamines were left on my car after every shift of employment. Despite the precautions I had taken to protect my location, a bomb that was designed to maximise damage but not completely destroy the vehicle (in order to complicate the insurance and finance burden) was placed into my car, which was parked beside my bedroom whilst I slept. A huge bunch of red roses were delivered to me, whilst the police were attending to take my statement and the inside of my car was still smouldering.

The emotional burden of realising I had been effectively "groomed" by my mother's widower, and subsequently having to navigate the process of divorce, brought forward the weight of a self-loathing I could never have imagined. My world became too heavy to bear.

For the first time in my life, I felt that I understood my mother and the emotional pain she must have been enduring to get to her decision. In addition, there was no-one to miss me, I had no-one. There was nothing to clutch to, I had nothing. Finally, the world and those in it no longer had to beat me into submission – I was willingly ready and able to end my own life. Finally, I could do something right and give the world what it had always wanted; my absence. The sheer relief of never enduring anything ever again was more than alluringly attractive. I not only welcomed, but desperately craved the finality of my immediate death.

Fast forward around 25 years and to the end of another legally binding relationship. This was the person who had stopped my first suicide attempt, had appointed themselves as "my protector" and consequently became what can only be described as my stalker. Although I had predominantly

The Power of Perspective

worked throughout the relationship, it was a restricted and isolated existence for me. Social interactions were done only with "permission" and I was often forbidden contact with the other person's family members when there were domestic disputes. During all disputes those I sought friendship or comfort from were exposed to a portion of toxic behaviours that were deemed intolerable for them.

The domestic situation had passed being what most would consider tolerable many years before. On the final night of the relationship, I had reached my point of "no return". I knew that I would be isolated from those who now held a deep-seated place in my heart, however the devastating effect of the cohabitation were now thrust upon them and unbearable to witness. As a result, I deemed myself as at least partially responsible for their exposure. Guilty that I was responsible for innocence being exposed to my gruesome reality, which they did not deserve.

During the previous 24 hours, the household had been sleep-deprived and I could bear it no longer. No-one was going to be let sleep whilst I remained present. Attempts to call law enforcement were thwarted, tyres were slashed to restrict my ability to leave. Eventually I made my way out of the home with begrudged police assistance and two suitcases of clothes. Five of my teeth were broken and being in an isolated area my options were limited. I was indeed back on my own with my suitcases and his words searing through the quiet neighbourhood and the drenching torrential rain that the only options I had were "to go and be a whore, or go kill yaself".

After the police arranged that I could have the use of a car that was not mine I was escorted to an isolated camping area where the police insisted on my assurance that I would not return to the situation. I promised them I had no intention of ever returning again. A kind person lent me $50 for fuel so I could return to a more familiar area.

Regardless of what transpired I knew I would never be returning to this relationship. When the thought of suicide entered my mind, I made a promise to myself that I would not, under any circumstances that I was about to endure, be killing myself. This person had taken and received all they ever would and despite their insistence that I was worthless, I now loathed someone more than myself. They most certainly were not worthy of holding the place of my grieving widow.

It took many years for me to come to the realisation that the first time I attempted suicide, and the moment I made the decision that I would not suicide, the circumstances in which these decisions were made were undeniably similar. The only difference was my perspective.

It was not that I had any more self-love, in fact I was ashamed, humiliated, defeated, exhausted and felt the familiar depths of devastation. I did come to the realisation that the existence I had lived was so unbearable, that I would rather be alive,

The Power of Perspective

on my own, in the middle of wherever with no-one, rather than continue an intolerable existence. If nothing else, I knew I could be worthless on my own.

In fact, it was necessary to utilise my self-loathing to punish myself into a better existence despite myself. I made a promise to myself that regardless of any circumstance I would make myself laugh everyday – even if that meant laughing at the enormity of the burden of my life.

Emotions – Recognise, Respect, Respond, Reflect, Release

As a child of a parent that has died by suicide, the world in which we are now left to navigate, relate to and function in, has beat our parents to a point of submission where they could no longer conceive being able to exist.

Memories of joy are now tinged with a hindsight of sadness and can trigger intrusive, unanswerable questioning around the legitimacy, truth and expression of emotions.

Most people can understand the difficulty in being able to empathise with, being angry at, or unable to forgive or accept; a drunk driver that selfishly killed your parent, a group of criminals that beat your parent to death or a multibillion-dollar company withholding money and resources on safe work practices whilst demanding maximum production that negligently led to the death of your parent.

Now imagine the effort in navigating the emotions, strategies and coping mechanisms of having to harmoniously exist and survive 24 hours a day, 7 days a week, 365 days per year in the same household as those killers listed. Most people would find this situation unfathomable and undoubtedly difficult to negotiate. Those forced into such a situation would inevitably experience anger at both the perpetrator and those with the power of forcing them into the situation of having to survive such a cohabitation.

When a parent commits the final act of suicide, that cohabitation scenario can now dominate the underlying essence of our existence.

Without the benefit of being able to identify a particular perpetrator to blame as discussed in a previous chapter, the anger becomes more widespread, generalised and spontaneous. The killer of our parent is invisible yet ever present, consisting of a generalised lack of empathy, support, compassion and an overwhelming feeling of failure to be able to function within, comply to and adequately satisfy personal, familial or societal demands and expectation.

It is easy to feel angered by a world that was too cruel for our parent to survive. Left to navigate a world in which all die but only some survive. The introduction of this knowledge

Emotions – Recognise, Respect, Respond, Reflect, Release

can detract from the joys available in living a life as opposed to a defensive and/or reactive existence in a bid to survive.

Our parents are role models. We learn, good and bad, from them. Core beliefs are often formed according to our exposure to our parents. In the aftermath of the suicide of our parent it is easy to justify the world as a cruel place and life as something to survive rather than a journey to enjoy.

Parental abandonment and/or neglect, intentional or by circumstance, in every form is likely to instigate overwhelming feelings of worthlessness, anger, confusion, frustration and despair. It is unlikely that any emotion identification and management skills will have been observed, practised, taught or acquired. An inability to recognise, respect, respond, reflect and release our emotions, hinders our ability to identify their associated sub-conscious behaviours.

Unaddressed emotions are like popcorn kernels sitting in your little pot belly waiting for the ignition on the stove. Unidentified emotion sits there, dormant, inactive, just waiting. A seemingly simple issue can ignite the stove and before you know it the popcorn is spilling over in a burst of anger that seems out of proportion to the issue at hand. The ignition may warrant a little bit of anger or frustration, however, when put in addition to what was in the pot, we have just created the perfect situation for an overflow. Rather than a slight frustration, there is a seething, destructive anger which needs to be released.

An awareness of the importance of emotion identification and management is an integral component of self-analysis and crucial for self-awareness and self-responsibility. An inability to appropriately respond to emotional needs within our experiences will inevitably produce an environment of emotional overwhelm.

The burden of emotional overwhelm is not exclusive to traumatic or life-altering event exposure. An unwillingness or inability to appropriately manage seemingly meaningless behaviours resulting from unaddressed emotions can ensure the "load we are bearing" becomes as overwhelming as a disastrous event. In fact, carrying the burden of many unaddressed emotions and their needs can be equally as debilitating. Many unaddressed emotional needs inevitably decreases the ability to manage the emotions of a traumatic and life-altering experience.

As an example, anger we feel toward our parent will often be directed subconsciously toward ourselves and/or those trying to relate to us. Acknowledging our anger toward our parent is difficult and can stir feelings of guilt, rejection, confusion and sadness, therefore it seems easier to justify the projection of that anger onto the world we are surrounded by.

Although our anger may be both understandable and perceived as justified, it must also be acknowledged, understood and released by the self. Without recognising and acknowledging anger we inevitably distinguish our ability to create, experience and sustain a life of joy, harmony or peace.

Unreleased anger hinders the ability to perceive acceptance. An inability to accept is a perception of rejection. A perception of rejection hinders the ability to reconcile. An inability to reconcile promotes a perception of helplessness. A perception of helplessness promotes a perception of powerlessness. A perception of powerlessness hinders the ability to practise self-discipline.

Most actions undertaken whilst angry provide an instant feeling of regret and/or despair. The repercussions of our actions whilst angry will have consequences. The only difference being that the consequences will vary in range from mild, short-term effects to devastating and life-altering. This in turn can create its own cycle of anger and frustration, justifying our perception of survival in an unjust world.

Anger as a dominating emotion negates the ability to practise empathy, compassion, kindness or consideration of the self and toward others. It is the apparent lack of these emotions that have contributed to the circumstances in which we have experienced parental abandonment.

Unreleased emotions will inevitably affect your relationship with others and with yourself. These emotions can then present issues of domestic and relational violence, abusive and criminal actions to persons or property, incarceration, substance abuse, self-harm, a decline in mental health fitness and physical well-being.

Allowing others to provoke sustained sub-conscious reactions from ourselves, inevitably negates our power of self-control and allows personal boundaries to be dictated by others. Your emotions become a self-punishment for another person's actions to yourself. You have alleviated them of responsibility by inflicting the consequence of their behaviour on yourself. In turn, you will be unwittingly inflicting unnecessary chaos on yourself and those around you.

This is not saying that emotion has no place, should never be experienced or expressed. On the contrary, every emotion has the capacity to be our greatest guide and teacher. Our behaviours are an expression of our emotions. Recognising the emotion for the lesson it is can be a very powerful skill.

It is with the consideration of this knowledge that we should endeavour to consciously ensure that adequate emotion management, resources and techniques are available, researched, thoughtfully considered and practised.

Fact is, every experience, whether it be exhilarating or traumatic and including the mundane, creates who we are as individuals. Many "parts", particularly those that have been born from painful or traumatic experiences, we endlessly wish did not exist. This perspective ensures we continue the traumatic experience, validating and keeping the intensity of the associated emotions in the present.

Emotions – Recognise, Respect, Respond, Reflect, Release

These emotions, thoughts and the associated sub-conscious processes are now part of the existing journey. They form the individual that we now are. It is our choice how to use them, such as a tool for self-loathing to justify self-sabotage or an opportunity to practice self-compassion and self-awareness.

When we allow an "experience" to utilise the same emotional energy as when it occurred in the past, we then validate the intensity of its presence in the present. Management of the perspective and the energy applied to the current experience, including the associated emotional intensity, is imperative in alleviating the debilitating and destructive effects of the past, in the present.

The core function of our emotions is to communicate to ourselves and to others. An inability or unawareness of the importance of emotion identification and management is conducive to a sub-conscious, behaviour-based, therefore reactive individual.

Reactive individuality creates an environment of entitlement. An entitled environment hinders an individual's ability to identify, accept or practice self-awareness and self-responsibility.

Identification, analysis and management of our emotions is essential to practice self-awareness and self-responsibility.

Self-awareness and self-responsibility are the most powerful tools we have as individuals in creating, promoting and maintaining personal, familial and societal relationships conducive to optimum mental health fitness.

Communication Needs Comprehension

"Sticks & stones can break my bones, but words will never hurt me." As popular as this statement may be, it is also devastatingly untrue. This is particularly the case for those that are not familiar with the idea that what people verbalise reflects the verbalising person, not those they are verbalising to. As empowering as this perception may be, it is not often a chosen perception for many.

Without doubt, words utilised throughout my early childhood had an enormous impact on the perception of myself, my perception of the world and my place in it. Many destructive, some intended and some not, words and phrases had a direct impact on my mental health development and fitness, hindering my ability to navigate healthy and beneficial relationships.

The truth is words do have impact. Words spoken to and around children have a lasting impact on forming perceptions of themselves, how to communicate to the world in which they exist and will have a direct impact on future intimate, familial and communal relations. Most of this will be absorbed and expressed subconsciously.

Many will accept that if a child is told throughout school that they are dumb, a failure or won't succeed, they are unlikely to obtain scholarly success without intervention or resources being applied on a conscious level. In fact, most parents would be furious if a teacher subjected their child to such intolerable and unacceptable behaviour yet communicate with their own child without conscious thought on the impact or in/comprehension of their own verbal and non-verbal communications.

The impact of our vocabulary and the importance of comprehension does not lessen as we grow older. Constant exposure to verbal abuse and toxic behaviours can be psychologically damaging. The impact on the receiving party can be traumatising and debilitating.

Likewise, this same vocabulary, with appropriate comprehension, can be used to effectively communicate for us and to enhance and elevate our relations with others.

The increasing prevalence of juvenile crime within the community is often met with social media outrage, disbelief,

Communication Needs Comprehension

suggestions of retaliatory actions, citizen rights and so on. The youth of our society are a broad reflection of the environments to which they have been exposed.

Children experience, observe and sub-consciously absorb human behaviour, without comprehension of the psychology promoting the behaviour to which they have been exposed to, or experienced. The inability to comprehend human behaviour negates the responsibility of self-accountability.

In general, children will be able to access, navigate and manage artificial intelligence and the internet before they acquire an understanding of the psychology of human behaviour or mental health management.

Exposure to, and acceptance of, toxic behaviours within our immediate environment, social surrounds and wider community without human psychology education or understanding, negates the formation of self-awareness and self-responsibility.

A lack of self-awareness and self-responsibility negates the perception of the necessity for self-discipline. The inability to navigate self-discipline promotes an environment of entitlement hindering the ability to navigate empathy or consideration for the self and others.

Children are not born with a vocabulary, they learn it. They are not born with a dictionary or thesaurus, they learn meaning and comprehension from witnessing interactions between and with their parents, guardians, family, community and the environments to which they are exposed. Comprehension of non-verbal communication is often a skill left for education through exposure and therefore will vary according to perception.

Prior to language capability, a child's observation, comprehension and perception of relations within their immediate environment are the basis on which the child will learn to display/hide appropriate/inappropriate behaviour, dependant on the perceived benefit/failure of the response to behaviours observed/displayed. If self-awareness and self-responsibility are not displayed/observed or consciously taught, the ability to grasp these concepts during early formation of the child self is hindered. The ability for the child to recognise and manage emotions will be impacted, hindering enhanced communication and social navigation skills.

We can liken the differing impact to a skilled tradesperson with complete education and knowledge prior to undertaking a job, to an uneducated and unskilled labourer doing the same job and learning as he goes. When compared, even if both have the determination to complete the job at hand, it is clear who is going to experience less complications throughout the job.

Words on their own are not effective communication. Often, we hear the phrase "communication is key". That being the

Communication Needs Comprehension

case means comprehension is the synonymous lock. The key and lock are most effective when used together.

Communication without comprehension is not only likely to be ineffective, but also reduce our effectiveness in navigating relations with ourselves and those with which we interact. Comprehension encourages understanding. An inability or unwillingness to comprehend negates any effective communication.

It is my experience that we yell, fight and argue only when we feel we are not being heard, considered or understood. What we choose to ignore is the fact that often, once we have entered the yelling phase, effective communication has been abandoned and comprehension of the initial subject is more likely to be misunderstood or negated completely.

It is possible to navigate effective communication strategies based on mutual understanding and consideration. Where we can effectively communicate our needs, concerns, desires and discomforts within relationships that possess an intent willingness to comprehend, we have effectively voided any necessity for argument.

Threats Must Have Consequences

The first time I had someone verbally threaten to kill themselves it was a painful shock. My experience with suicide so far had been very real. Each suicide, including my attempts and the pact arrangement (except for the pact partner) had to that point been deliberately covered, silently planned, and actioned without announcement. Thwarted attempts had been discovered by chance without prior warning of the potential discovery.

After scrambling out of the shock, I felt an intense anger at the threat. How dare you threaten me, having the knowledge of my experiences!

Verbalised during a somewhat trivial domestic altercation, the threat was delivered with coercive control, emotional

Seats of Suicide

blackmail, and manipulation. If the suicide was attempted and successful, I would be responsible; for the death, for the repercussion to the loved ones, for the children that would lose their parent. Could I live with that?

The anger turned to fear. People do suicide, so maybe it wasn't a threat. How did you know?

The fear melded with shame. Would confrontation be the determining factor that pushed them over that edge? Did I even have the right to be angry?

The shame merged with guilt. Was it me? Did I bring this world of suicide on them? This person once saved me from an attempt; is this how they felt? I hadn't wanted to be saved, yet I had been, so was I now obligated to return the favour? The loved ones referred to had provided me with a variety of assistance and unofficial counselling, so didn't I now owe them a similar courtesy?

I empathised, pleaded, rationalised, agreed to demands and promised to keep the episode secret so others would not need to carry the burden of worry in return for a promise that the circumstances would never be repeated.

The threats were repeated, many times.

After many years, the threats had become tiring. After receiving pictures of a noose ready to go and the usual barrage of texts of intent while I was physically unable to attend, professional intervention was called in. Police called in a Special Response Squad and the individual was hospitalised under a mandatory order. The process was different to a civilian report and the individual was forced to face some unwanted consequences to obtain release.

It became clear after this incident that for this individual, they were indeed simply threats used for manipulation and therefore the threats became obsolete. The repercussions from the threats remained.

When an individual does not receive the response to the manipulation as they intended but instead receives an appropriate medical response, the threat is no longer an effective tool for manipulation, control or shame.

In the event that the individual was serious about the threat of intent, responding by seeking professional intervention ensures you have also provided the individual with an opportunity to address the underlying mental health issues they are experiencing as overwhelming. Although this does not mean they will address their underlying emotions, you have provided an opportunity for them to do so.

Secrecy and repeated tolerance around suicidal ideations creates an environment where being the acceptor of these behaviours is to become an enabler of the behaviours. Enabling these behaviours is as destructive as the behaviours themselves. In accepting the destructive behaviours, the mental health of all individual beings exposed to the behaviours will be impacted.

Suicidal threats by their very nature are manipulative, exploitive and an attempt to force control in what is perceived to be uncontrollable circumstances. They are a clear indication that the individual delivering the threat has lost control of their mental health wellbeing, unable (at least temporarily) to grasp a concept of self-awareness or self-responsibility.

To be tolerant of and ignorant to these behaviours without an appropriate response is an indicator that the tolerator also has some mental health fitness analysis required in order to ascertain why they feel the need to allow themselves to be manipulated and controlled in this manner.

Repeated suicidal ideations without attempts to seek professional intervention or assistance is, at the very least, psychological abuse.

Acceptance of repeated suicidal ideations without attempt to seek professional intervention is psychological abuse and enabling toxic relations.

Enabling toxic relations is supporting the detrimental impact to the mental health of every individual exposed to the corresponding destructive behaviours of such relations. The impact will be familial, communal and generational.

Threats Must Have Consequences

Seeking assistance for an individual that is unable/unwilling to seek assistance for themselves is not a rejection of the person making the threat. Seeking professional intervention and resources is not a betrayal or judgement on the individual. On the contrary, seeking help, resources and intervention is the most appropriate response to any individual that is enduring the burden of a mental health crisis.

If you were all the "help" they needed, then the situation in which the individual felt compelled to make the threat itself would never have eventuated.

The perception of shame, embarrassment and the complexity in obtaining such resources is yet another mental health challenge and further evidence that humanity itself is refusing to grasp the complexity of being a human, with little to no education on what it is to be a human being.

Conscious Change

Although change can often bring loss, discouragement, criticism and be challenging, any form of forward movement can only be obtained by change. Change can also be enlightening, invigorating, rewarding, joyous, pleasant and peaceful. When change is thrust upon us through external circumstances, we can experience overwhelming emotions exacerbated by uncertainty and unfamiliarity.

Some may say they crave, need or desire change, yet be unwilling to instigate any action to create the change they profess to desire.

Others may often be seen to be "trying" to change yet find the obstacles insurmountable.

The most perplexing conversations I have had around change is when one insists that they *did* change, but the response/

reaction they received was not what they wanted/expected/required to the "change". The "change didn't work" so previous language/behaviours were then brought back into the interaction.

Change by its very definition is to modify, alter or become different. To be different, is to be not the same, distinct, or separate.

Therefore, if you instigate a change, yet revert to an original behaviour, then an actual change has never taken place. It's akin to believing you dived into a pool and drowned, when in fact, you only stuck your toe in the water and felt like you were drowning. The experience and outcome are distinctly and irrefutably incomparable.

Often when we set out to instigate change, we inadvertently set ourselves up for failure by having or expecting unrealistic achievable leaps which inevitably result in failing to achieve the outcome so desired. This process can be subconsciously repeated in order to justify a perception that change is difficult, or to justify a fear/acceptance of a perception of failure.

In order to negate this process, it is imperative that we approach change itself with a focus on our perspective to the nature of change. We make change consciously achievable.

When we achieve change even in the most miniscule form, we change our perception of our ability to change. The more resistant we are to change or the more fearful we are of failure, the more we need to focus on the feeling of achieving change and not the change itself.

For example, if we desired to reduce a sugar intake of four sugars per beverage, an immediate reduction of three sugars is likely to be rejected by our palate. We decrease the likelihood of success and increase our perception of expected failure when we revert to the four sugars. Instead, by gradually reducing grains of sugar, we increase the likelihood of inevitable success. The palate barely noticed the gradual reduction of grains and each grain is an achievement. Any sense of conviction to implementing this gradual change will eventually have your palate rejecting the four sugar beverages.

Change becomes achievable. Our perception of failure to grasp change can be adjusted to an opportunity to amend the method of approach to any desired change, rather than an obstacle to change itself.

We can find ourselves desiring change without understanding the actual change we desire. Unexpected change can be thrust upon us through life experiences forcing change. This often requires that we focus on the most basic, simplest and miniscule change that we can identify. It is imperative that the changes we set to achieve be broken into segments so achievable that failure is only obtainable by an intent to not change.

We are unable to change others, nor do we have the right to. If we have the perception that we can change another human being, we must also recognise that others would also have a right to change us as they perceive. Most would find this to be an unjust exertion of power over us as individuals. We can, however, provide others with support, encouragement and opportunity to change.

When we change, such as being consciously responsive as opposed to subconsciously reactive, we instigate change around us. Those that endeavour to relate to us in the same manner now receive a conscious response as opposed to the predictive reaction as experienced in previous interactions. We have therefore changed the interaction, regardless of the individual we are interacting with.

The decision to consciously change ourselves as desired/required must be full and complete. Without the required conscious commitment to achievable change, we increase the likelihood of failure to change. This provides a subconscious justification of the resistance to change as previously believed/imagined.

Age Appropriate

Throughout my life and the writing of this book, I have had the opportunity to bear witness to the confusion around age appropriateness, including the consequential impacts to be navigated for those directly affected by government authority and parental decisions in relation to age-appropriate knowledge.

A lack of communication that has the intention of protecting those "not old enough" can create confusion, frustration and anger. When a child has an awareness of a situation and is unable to receive adequate communication and comprehension, we can then be presented with feelings of inadequacy, withdrawal and mistrust. This complicates the issue further and may hinder the healing process. If the situation exposed to is traumatic in nature, the lack of communication and response may compound the extent of the trauma experienced.

In simple terms, if a child is enduring an experience or exposure, the conceptual communication of the experience is imperative during the experience.

In entertaining the perspective that our children learn from their familial, communal, societal and worldly exposure and experiences, it becomes appropriate to observe the mass perception of these environments and the consequential impacts of exposure-based learning.

The ever-present issue of bullying within the education system is a prime example of a species that has an inability or unwillingness to acknowledge the importance in educating their young prior to or during exposure, of its own species' basic psychology and behaviour principles.

Human psychology is largely deemed as an optional occupation or profession in adult life, rather than an underlying basic requirement of every human existence.

Governments make decisions based purely on economics. The education system adheres to government guidelines which provide information and education for individuals on how to conform to and function within the societal economic system. Education on human psychology and behaviour is not the dominant function of these systems and is predominantly reduced to an individual learning based on exposure and perceptual experience within these environments.

Age Appropriate

It is unlikely that a member of the human species can undertake a journey within the societal education system without some form of exposure to bullying, whether it be the bully, the bullied or the witness to such behaviours. Personally, I have experienced all three positions.

The mental health impact of bullying behaviour is well documented, researched, acknowledged and recognised. Yet for generations, the "unacceptable" behaviour has continued to be accepted and the "intolerable" impact is tolerated.

The general mass perception of the influence and power of a bully suggest that they are superior in strength, dominance, intelligence and/or popularity. This mass perception ensures the continuance of unacceptable behaviours being accepted, and the intolerable impact of such behaviours tolerated. The perception of benefit to a potential bully remains desirable. Individuals that have a desire to experience the perceived benefits of such behaviours will continue the behaviour whilst the recognition is perceived as beneficial and/or desirable.

The behaviours displayed by bullies are sub-conscious reactions to feelings associated with perceptions of inadequacy, worthlessness, rejection, inferiority and instability. Whilst the behaviours are deemed worthy of benefit in negating these undesirable feelings and perceptions, the behaviours will continue.

In experiencing emotions, reactions, behaviours and various exposures void of understanding or explanation, we endeavour to interpret the encounter or situation with limited knowledge, experience and perception. The environment is exposure-based learning and allows for limited perceptual capabilities, susceptible to mass-perception and peer influence.

In obtaining an understanding of human behaviours and the corresponding possibility of emotions that underlie the behaviour, both the response to and perceived benefit of the behaviour changes. No longer perceived as a position of strength, the behaviour of the bully is now understood by its peers as a human experiencing a lack of self-acceptance and fulfilment. The behaviour of a bully is no longer perceived as strong, dominant, powerful or popular. The behaviour can become understood for the mental health imbalance and perception of need that it displays. The whole purpose of the bully becomes destabilised. The perception of benefit of such behaviours becomes negated.

Most of us, throughout our childhood, will have been exposed to "wordly truths". As we mature into adolescence, we come to realise these "truths" are not quite truthful. Whilst this is done under a guise of allowing childhood innocence, realistically the good intent has increasingly rolled into a world size scale of commercialisation that increasingly promotes a sense of entitlement or disadvantage depending on the economic social status of one's family connections.

Age Appropriate

For many, the childhood innocence we deem so important has already been devastated by exposure to toxic relations and exposures that are more debilitating than any lack of fantasy belief could ever be.

In equipping our young during their formative years with an understanding of their own emotions, reactive emissions and associated behaviours, we widen the scope for self-awareness, self-worth, self-discipline, self-responsibility and therefore self-acceptance.

In promoting self-acceptance, we promote an environment of understanding and empathy.

An environment of understanding and empathy allows for freedom of expression, vulnerability and self-empowerment.

An environment that promotes self-empowerment, through self-awareness, self-acceptance and self-responsibility, is integral in optimising relational awareness and mental health resilience amongst our species.

My Head – My Harmony
(Self-Awareness)

Being that I am the only person with complete access to me in my entirety, I oversee the process of ensuring harmonious mental health. I have the choice to actively manage my connections, interactions and relations with myself and others. Listening, interpreting and responding to my thoughts, hearing my responses to those I communicate with, learning to interpret my emotions, manage my behaviours, seeking assistance as required, searching for and utilising resources, and reaching out for help, are my responsibility and within my power.

My Body – My Boundaries
(Self-Worth)

I have full authorisation of my body. I can establish, enforce and maintain control of my body and its use. I have the choice in all physical and energetic interactions. I have the choice to nourish or deplete. I have the choice to strengthen or weaken my physical, emotional and energetic boundaries. It is my responsibility to interpret the messages of my body and respond to its needs.

My Response – My Responsibility
(Self-Discipline)

It is my responsibility to understand and manage how I respond to myself, my environment, those around me and my experiences. I have the choice to be active in my response or thoughtlessly reactive. I choose the quality and quantity of my interaction with myself, my environment and actively manage my relations with others.

My Journey – My Job
(Self-Responsibility)

The purpose of my natural existence is to utilise my presence and navigate my experience. I have the choice on the quality, quantity and interpretation of my experiences. I am responsible for the quality of care I provide for myself regardless of external circumstance. I am responsible for my thoughts, behaviours, impact and personal growth. Being the only competitor on my journey, I experience my journey at my pace.

Not Choosing Is A Choice
(Self-Acceptance)

When it is time for your fruit to fall from the tree, you can choose to go on the quest to figure out how to extract the seed and nurture an orchard to create a source of lasting nutrition or you can throw it on the ground to attract insects, be infested with maggots, watch it rot and endure the stench of its demise.

For the fruit perishing whilst still dependant on the tree, please remember, even rotting fruit has a seed at its core willing and able to bear fruit given the correct environment.

To Purchase Merchandise

Or to Contact The Author

Please Visit

www.jmmurray.com.au

Reflections

Seats of Suicide

Reflections

Seats of Suicide

Reflections

www.ingramcontent.com/pod-product-compliance
Lightning Source LLC
Chambersburg PA
CBHW040243130526
44590CB00050B/4280